Anyone can entertain a winner ….

But few can create winning entertainment!

Leader of Gaming Innovation

For the 21st century

New Casino Slots

How to Play
•
Have Fun
•
And WIN!

Victor H. Royer

iUniverse, Inc.
New York   Bloomington

New Casino Slots
How to Play • Have Fun • And WIN!

iUniverse books may be ordered through booksellers or by contacting:

iUniverse
1663 Liberty Drive
Bloomington, IN 47403
www.iuniverse.com
1-800-Authors (1-800-288-4677)

Because of the dynamic nature of the Internet, any Web addresses or links contained in this book may have changed since publication and may no longer be valid. The views expressed in this work are solely those of the author and do not necessarily reflect the views of the publisher, and the publisher hereby disclaims any responsibility for them.

ISBN: 978-1-4502-3801-4 (pbk)
ISBN: 978-1-4502-3802-1 (ebk)

Printed in the United States of America

iUniverse rev. date: 6/3/2010

Contents

Foreword

This is my 22nd book on casino games and casino slots. In this new book, I will introduce you to some of the world's greatest slot machines, the ones that can be found in the modern casinos of the 21st century.

Much has happened in the world of technological innovation in the past decade, including many advances in the world of casino slots. You are about go on an incredible journey featuring selections of the most innovative casino slot machines offered by Aristocrat Technologies Inc. The games in this book are by no means the only ones you'll find in your favorite casino, but they are the cutting edge examples of the best in video slots and new stepper games. These are the slot machines you may see in casinos now, as well as those you will see in the coming years. There is timeless information available here that will serve you well for all your visits to the casino, and all your choices in selecting the best casino video slot machines now available, and those that you will find in the future.

As I am writing this book, it is March 2010. The most recent gaming convention in Las Vegas has just finished, and the world's leading manufacturers of casino slots have previewed the kind of great new games you will soon be playing. This book will help you choose from among all of those machines that you find in your favorite casino. You will therefore be able to focus directly on those games that I am describing in this book, and consequently be able to play them immediately, without having to learn how to play them while using your own money in the casino. One of the main reasons why I have decided to write this book is to do precisely that—to give you an opportunity to shorten the learning curve, to find the good games right away, and to know how to play them to their optimum advantage, and for your best possible entertainment.

The new slot machines in the casinos of the 21st century are nothing like the slots that we all used to play. I still remember coming to Las Vegas many years ago and playing the 3-reel clunkers that took a silver dollar in a slot at the top and had a heavy handle on the side. The reels were weighted with lead weights which caused the mechanism to stop them in turn, from left to right, each with a loud clang as it came to a stop, displaying the fruit symbol—or a bar—on the small window at the front of the machine. You got a good workout pulling those handles, and if you were a regular player you could develop some musculature in your biceps and forearms, not to mention the strong grip in your wrist as you grabbed onto that one-armed bandit to pull its handle. And when you won something the machine would release a gush of coins that poured out like a torrent into a tiny tray at the bottom, often spilling on the floor in front of you.

I still remember the feeling of awe the first time I saw coins pouring out of that machine. It made a loud racket as the coins fell into the metal tray and bounced around every which way. That was the beginning of my personal love affair with the world of slots. I have never forgotten that feeling, and how awesome Las Vegas seemed to me at that time, with all the glitz, neon, and glamour associated with the gambling capital of the world.

But times have changed. Those old clunkers are long gone, relegated to museums and gift shops selling olden-style slots and other historical paraphernalia. The slots themselves have undergone several generations of evolution, from purely mechanical and electromechanical in the 1980s to computerized in the 1990s and then to fully computerized slots in the early part of the 21st century. Today, all slot machines—no matter how they may look—are computerized. They run on a computer chip inside of which is a virtual reel table that decides which combinations will be selected among the random choices made possible by the computer program, and something which is commonly referred to as the Random Number Generator. The symbols you see on the reels are, therefore, merely graphic representations of sequences of binary numerals which are part of the computer programs that run these slot machines, the selected combinations of which are then transmitted to the graphic interface and displayed on the screen. Consequently, what you now understand as reel slots—those that have spinning barrels—have similar computerized principles just as the video reel games.

There are thousands of different kinds of slot machines on the casino floor of the 21st century. They are made by several well-known manufacturers, among whom is Aristocrat Technologies, one of the premier innovative designers and suppliers of new video slot machines and stepper games. Aristocrat, headquartered in Australia, now has a strong presence in the United States as well as in the entire world. They have introduced the kind of machines and games that have become known as "Australian-style slots." Before Aristocrat, slots were generally thought to have evolved as far as possible. But those who had the vision—the founders and innovators who created the Aristocrat company—realized that casino slot machines do not have to be "just the same old thing." They took the concept of slot machines—called "pokies" in Australia—and developed an all-encompassing experience of casino entertainment which brought not only the world of gambling to the playing of these slots, but also the world of entertainment. These games are not just entertaining, they are also gambling games perfect for casino adult entertainment. They provide wins, and they provide a multitude of bonusing experiences that not only enhance the games themselves, but specifically permit you to have great longevity at the machine while experiencing the full benefit and advantage of such modern 21st century casino technology.

It is for these reasons, as well as many others, that Aristocrat slot machines—available as both video slots and as the more traditional 5-reel and 3-reel stepper slots—have proven popular not only in Australia, but throughout the casinos in the United States, including those in Las Vegas, Reno, Atlantic City, and the Indian and tribal casinos, as well as in most of the major gaming centers of the world. Today, just about everywhere in the world you will be able to find an Aristocrat slot machine, and therefore be able to use this book and know which games to look for, and why.

In the chapters that follow I showcase many of these great games and explain some of the terminology that is now necessary, and has become common, in the language of casino entertainment. I will explain what is meant by "Multi Line," what is meant by Aristocrat's "Reel Power®" and "*Hyperlink®*" categories, what is meant by "MSP," or "multi-denomination," or "Standalone Progressives," and many other such terms and statements that are important to understand if you are to maximize your entertainment on the casino slots you may choose to play. I also provide photographs of many of these great games, including the separate game screens, bonus screens, and other such events that are part of almost all of the modern casino slots. There are primary games, often called "base games," and features that include second-screen bonuses, free games, mystery jackpots, scatter pays, and other "extras" that make the world of modern casino slots not just more fun, but very often the best investment for your entertainment experience.

And the best news about these great new casino slots? Most of them are single-penny games. On many of these games, to purchase 1-payline requires only 1-cent in American money. Games like this are collectively known as "penny games," although you should understand that many of them have multiple lines and therefore usually the minimum play requirement for the maximum benefit is at least that many lines. For example, if the machine has 25 lines, your initial minimum bet to activate all of the lines—which is always my best advice—will be 25-cents. And, of course, there are machines which have many more lines than that, including those that have ante bets, and other options that you may select depending on your particular perspective, desire, goal, and play choices and options.

Personally, I always like to play maximum credits and maximum number of lines on any slot machine I play. That is my preference, because I want to win as much as I can and have the chance to achieve the biggest bang for my buck every time I play. I understand, though, that many people come to the casino for "the great casino experience"; they want to spend as much time as possible at the casino slots of their choice in order to maximize their enjoyment and entertainment experience. Because of that, in this book I also provide the knowledge necessary for you to be able to play frugally, while at the same time gaining the maximum value and entertainment from the experience. Playing casino slots in the 21st century is not just a passive exercise of walking into the casino and dropping your money in any slot machine you happen to walk past. Now more than ever it is up to you, the player, the customer, to look for the best games available to you—and to know how to play them before investing your money. And that too is part of this book, this guide to the games in the modern casino.

Finally, my purpose in writing this book is show you how to enhance your entertainment. I am in no way suggesting, or recommending, that you go to the casino with money you cannot afford to lose, or expect that you will somehow find the magic answer to your financial problems by gambling for a living, on slot machines or any other casino game. While it is possible to become a professional gambler, it is also my purpose in this book to let you know, in no uncertain manner, that all casino slots—with the possible exception of some skill-based games—are mathematically programmed to hold a certain percentage for the casino, and as such are therefore mathematically unbeatable. This may sound ominous, and it may seem as if I am telling you that you can never win on a slot machine. That is absolutely not the case! I personally have won many jackpots on slot machines, including those that I feature in this book, but I would be remiss if I did not point out to you, in all truthfulness, transparency, clarity, and understanding, that this book and any advice I mention in it is in no way to be understood as some kind of a "get rich quick scheme" for beating the casino slots, either those described in this book, or others you may choose to play.

My purpose is to show you which casino slots I think are among the best, to explain how they work, to show you how to play them, to help you make the best choices in maximizing your enjoyment and, of course, to show you how to make your casino visit a profitable one—to help you to choose the best casino slot machine for your entertainment, and to show you how you can increase your chance of WINNING! After all, winning is an inherent and important part of any casino slot machine. If no casino slot machine ever paid anything, no one would play them. Then there would be no slot machines, there would be no casinos, and there would be no need for books such as this one. It is a proven fact that casino slots *do* pay, that they *do* hit jackpots, and that by playing them correctly your chance of wins are increased. But you must understand that to be profitable, you must approach playing modern casino slots empowered with the knowledge that is provided in this book as well as the skills necessary to extract the maximum enjoyment from playing the machines you choose to play. And then you must play them wisely.

While reading this book you will learn how to choose the best machines and games, how to play them properly and wisely and for your maximum benefit and enjoyment, giving yourself the best chance to experience not just the maximum entertainment value for your investment, but also the best possible chance for the greatest possible win. And when you do have such wins, take them home with you. You may not know this, but according to various published surveys (including the annual LVCVA survey, and those appearing in CEM magazine, as well as those conducted by my company), of all the people who play casino slots in Las Vegas some 86% are winners. So, you may ask, how is it that the casinos can make profits from slot machines? The answer is simple: The majority of people who win on casino slots don't take the wins back home with them. They put it back. Or, which is often the case, they play other games, perhaps craps, perhaps blackjack, perhaps other slots; they bet on sports or spend the money on food, shows, or other such entertainment options available in modern casino resorts. Is this wrong? Absolutely not. What you do with your own money is your business. My goal in this book is to show you how you can maximize the value for the money you choose to spend by selecting the casino slots wisely and knowing how to play them well, so that you may enjoy the wins that all of this knowledge—and your now-acquired skills and game selection abilities—make possible. And that's entertainment!

The Language of Casino Slots

When I first arrived in Las Vegas casinos, playing slots was still very simple: Put a coin in the slot, pull the handle, and see if you won. The new world of the 21st century casino slots is a giant leap forward, one that often leaves many players somewhat mystified. While these new games can look complicated, in reality they are just evolutionary successors to those very simple slots which were my first introduction into the world of casino gaming. Although in most cases we no longer use coins—because in most modern machines we now use currency validators and tickets instead of coins—the basic principle of the slot machine is still the same: You insert your currency, select the denomination, choose the number of lines and credits you want to play, and then push the play button and see if you won. Yes, there are a few more steps to this process than with the old slots, but the concept is the same. Nevertheless, every player should understand the language of modern casino slots. By understanding it—what it means, and how it affects the game play on the machine and games chosen—you, the player, enhance not only your overall enjoyment and entertainment, but also your financial decisions and your potential wins.

In this chapter, I will explore some of the most common terminology that applies to the modern slots that you will find in the casinos you choose to visit, particularly as those terms apply to the games and machines that I am featuring throughout this book. Think of this chapter as a kind of "dictionary" or a "language guide" that will help you not only to understand what this terminology means, but also how it relates directly to the games you will find in the modern casinos, and may choose to play. This terminology is not difficult to understand, but to my knowledge it has not appeared in any other book about casino slots. I shall therefore empower you with information that will help you make the most of your casino slot experience. The section that now follows briefly describes the meaning of each such terms, presented in no particular order, but shown as their own individual subheads. We begin with the most important of all, and that is the meaning of Multi Line.

Multi Line simply means "more than one line." Modern casino video slot games utilize line combinations across the reels to award wins. There can be any number of lines—9 lines, 20 lines, 25 lines. There are, of course, many other slot machines that have different numbers of lines. For example, the more "traditional" 3-reel and 5-reel stepper machines—the kind that look like the old ones with the handle to pull—may have only 1 payline across the screen, left to right. Other reel machines may have 3 pay lines across the screen with the standard payline in the middle, another payline at the top, and one more at the bottom. Some other machines—including video slots—may have 5 paylines, which usually include the basic 3 paylines across the screen left to right and then a "V format" with one payline forming the V in the same way as it is written here, and the 5th payline being an upside down version of this V. That is an example of the classic 5 paylines slot machine screen. Many video slots also employ this Multi Line format, and it is also popular in many of the higher denomination slots. Still other slot machines, of which many of the modern video slots are examples, may have many more paylines. The most common are 20 line, 25 line, 30 line, 50 line and 100 payline video slots. I show many of those later in this book.

The 50 Line game category showcases a multitude of spinning line combinations, including some of the newest titles such as *Lucky Leopard*™ and *Aloha Paradise*™. Because the 50 Line games were so popular, Aristocrat developed an exciting library of 100 Line games, including new titles such as *Sirena's Gold*™ and *Jackpot Manor*™. Most of these 50 Line and 100 Line games are available in two versions. In the first category are what is called 1-credit-buys-1-payline, while in the second category there are options traditionally called 1-credit-buys-2-paylines. This means that you may see the same game in a casino with different line options.

If you like to gamble, you will probably look for the kinds of machines and games, and denominations, that permit you to buy the most numbers of lines for the most number of credits in the highest possible denomination. Alternatively, if your enjoyment is primarily derived from spending a lot of time at the machine to experience all of its features, you may want to look for machines where you can buy two paylines with 1-credit, giving you a greater range of potential wins and bonuses. It all comes down to your own personal preference. In this chapter I will provide you with such information, so that you know what all of this means, and can then make your own informed choices.

Reel Power® games are exclusive to Aristocrat, and offer you the ability to purchase reels rather than lines. With a 3 x 5 reel format, you have up to 243 ways to win. Some of Aristocrat's newest *Reel Power*® games include *Chicken2*™, and *Party in Rio*™. This can be a somewhat tricky concept to understand.

Traditionally, when you play a line game and choose to play 10 lines, you do this by pressing the button marked "play 10 lines." You are then given the choice of selecting the number of credits you wish to play for each of these active paylines. For example, if you wish to play 1-credit per each selected payline, your total wager for these choices will be 10-credits, or 10c. But that machine—and others like it—gives you the choice of many more paylines. In the above example, if it were a 20-line game you would then be able to choose to activate up to that many lines, meaning 20 paylines total.

But on the *Reel Power*® games the situation is different. Here you are not purchasing additional paylines by wagering additional credits, you are instead purchasing additional *playing reels*. This means that on *Reel Power*® games there are *no paylines*, because for each reel that you purchase, by wagering additional credits, you are buying *all* of the possible symbol combinations on the highlighted reels. In a nutshell, this means that all symbols act as if they were "scatters" (symbols that pay anywhere on the screen), but they must be on adjacent reels from left to right. Therefore, to win, you *don't* need paylines, but you *do* need the winning symbols to be on the reels next to each other, left to right, in the highlighted area. The only exceptions are the "scatter" symbols which can win in any position anywhere, as described on each of the specific games. You will be able to see this in the chapters on the actual games, where I will show you the photos of each game, and also the game screens.

Xtra Reel Power™ builds on the popular Aristocrat *Reel Power*® game category, and is presented in a 4 x 5 reel format. This effectively gives you up to 1,024 ways to win. This concept is available in titles such as *Buffalo*™, *Timber Wolf*™ and *In the Gold*™. Aristocrat also offers a series of brand new 4 x 5 reel barrel-spinning slot machines—called "steppers" in industry lingo—which are also *Xtra Reel Power*™ games, offered on the *Viridian RFX Stepper*™ cabinet, featuring new games such as *Old Bayou*™ and *Salmon Rapids*™. These work on the same principle: You are buying reels instead of paylines, and as a result the winning combinations do not have to line up on any payline. They all function similarly to scatters across all adjacent active reels from left to right. It's a great way to enjoy a terrific variety of new slots.

Power Pay™ is a concept that uses the idea of an additional wager—commonly called the "ante" bet—with which you may be familiar if you have played some of the new table games in casinos. Basically, this is an additional wager you can choose to make in order to unlock more winning possibilities, as well as bonuses. This ante bet is akin to a bonus wager, such as those you may find in the table games Fortune Pai Gow Poker, or Let It Ride, both of which have been on the casino floor for a long time. While these games are not slot machines, and I mention them only as examples of the "bonus bet," or "side wager," the principle is similar to that now being used in some of these new slots. In those two table games I am using as examples, you can wager an additional amount—in a circle shown on the table layout—that pays you a bonus win in the event certain hands are achieved. On *Power Pay*™ slots, the ante bet is such an additional bonus pay feature that allows you to wager additional credits for additional pays, bonuses, and higher wins.

Naturally, there are differences among the many games offering this particular feature, but Aristocrat's *Power Pay*™ brand includes all of the new ante bet style games. When playing the *Power Pay*™ ante bet, you gain access to additional features in each game, such as free games, multipliers, re-spins and enhanced bonus game play. *Power Pay*™ also delivers a variable increase in the base payback and creates a more feature-rich and entertaining gaming experience. Some of the newest *Power Pay*™ titles include *Fire Light*™, *Golden Axe*™ and *Money Tree II*™.

Also based on the ante bets concept, *Bonus Bank* is Aristocrat's revolutionary random bonusing product. It delivers frequent and affordable bonus features to players who wager the extra ante bet. The popular *Mr. Cashman*®, *Lil' Lucy*® and *Money Honey*® characters are all part of the *Bonus Bank* lineup.

Standalone Progressives (SAP) are games with a single-level jackpot on screen. *Double Standalone Progressives* (DSAP) have a 2-level jackpot in the top box, and *Triple Standalone Progressives* (TSAP) have a 3-level jackpot in the top box. All three of these types of jackpot progressive games give you the opportunity to win these jackpot prizes, in addition to all of the pays available on the base game itself. Some additions to the Aristocrat standalone progressive library include *Elephant Trail*™, *Nile Princess*™ and *Sun & Moon*® *Total Eclipse* progressives, as well as brand new titles under the *Banana King*® and *Cashman Tonight*® designs.

A three-level jackpot with specially designed graphic sequences running in a themed signage and LCD top boxes, combined with high performing Aristocrat games, adds a new and exciting dimension to 21st century casinos. The *Xtreme Mystery*® concept gives your favorite casino the ability to reward many players who are playing games connected to the link. You can receive any one of the three growing jackpots at any time, on any of the Aristocrat machines you may be playing, as long as it is connected to the *Xtreme Mystery*® link. *Xtreme Mystery*® is now available on the Aristocrat *GEN7*™ platform, with new themes such as *Sky Heroes*™ and *Island Delight*®, all with a variety of different kinds of jackpots.

Bonus Bet™ includes any Aristocrat games that have an additional wager to play for the chance to win a progressive jackpot or major prize. Linked products like *Bank Buster*® and *Jackpot Deluxe*® are examples of Bonus Bet games. The newest additions to the family of *Bonus Bet Jackpot*™ games include the terrific *Hit the Heights*® and *Beat the Bandits*® themes. For example, *Hit the Heights*® is an entirely new series of 4 games with bonus games, a unique "wheel" bonus feature, and a topper that stands more than 3 feet high! This creates a huge presence on any casino floor, and is therefore instantly identifiable—making it easy for you to spot. (I will write more about this game later on in this book.) The *Beat the Bandits*® game features a 3-level progressive jackpot, and a top award mystery jackpot, where you can choose the level of jackpot you want to win. (More about this game too, in later chapters.)

Multi-Site Progressives

Aristocrat's Multi-Site Progressive games are those with one or more "life changing" jackpots that can be won, over multiple sites and/or states, depending on the various regulations in your particular gaming jurisdiction. Basically, these are the kind of games that can often provide you with multi million dollar wins, which to most people are certainly "life-changing" jackpots. Many familiar titles among such available games are the popular *Loco Loot®*, *Millioni$er®*, and the fully Asian-themed link *Fa Fa Fa Fortune King™*. The newest addition is *Mega Millioni$er®*, a *GEN7™*-driven Multi-Site Progressive where you can win a minimum of $1 million in GLI jurisdictional markets, and a minimum of $2 million in Nevada.

Hyperlink® is a patented linked progressive developed by Aristocrat. Groups of several gaming machines—called "banks"—are all linked together to jointly fund a randomly triggered four-level jackpot, available at any time to any player playing any machine in such a bank. One of the distinguishing features of the *Hyperlink®* concept occurs when the jackpot is triggered at random, and players then move into a second screen feature to determine what level of the jackpot is won.

Aristocrat continues to expand the licensed brand category with new themes like *Kentucky Derby*™ and *Jeff Foxworthy*™. The *Zorro*® games have been a favorite with players for many years, and *The Sopranos*® games are also a big hit. *JAWS*™, with its unique game play and bonus features, is quite distinctive, and can now be found in your favorite casino. "Licensed products" simply means that these games are based on themes, characters, ideas, or graphics that are famous, well-known, or have become part of pop-culture, and which are owned by their creators or copyright and trademark owners—individuals, or companies, other than the manufacturer of the slot machine. For example, Jeff Foxworthy owns the rights to his name and the comic characters he has developed. By signing an agreement with Aristocrat, he has provided a "license" to use his image, likeness, and characters, in the creation of the slot machine that bears his name. And this is similar to other such games whose main themes, or ideas, are based on products other than those created by Aristocrat directly. Perhaps the best way to understand it is this: If you create something, then it is yours. But if you can't make it yourself, and someone else comes to you and asks you for permission to make it, and you agree, then you have granted them a "license" to do this. That is what "licensed products" means.

The *Player's World*™ brand has a variety of multi game packs available on both standalone and linked games. The newest packs to join the *Player's World*™ family include *Player's World Ultimate*™, a low-line, multi-denominational pack featuring 2 exciting games, *Rhino Thunder*™ and *Super Bucks III*™. *Player's World Gold*™, a 4-game pack under *Mega Millioni$er*® and *Player's World Legends*™, a 4-game pack under *Cash Express*®, all add variety to these exciting linked products.

This means that one machine contains several games from which you can choose. It is basically the "menu concept" with which you may already be familiar, because it is the same as the choices available on many existing machines—and particularly on the newest interactive video slots—where the main screen displays a menu of choices, from which you can then choose the game you want to play. You make this choice by touching the screen over that game's icon. The machine then launches the game and all of its features for you to play. Some of these machines may only have 2 games from which to choose, others may have 4 games, and soon perhaps more. The concept is very simple: Just touch the screen over the game you wish to play!

Multi-Denomination

This is one of those terms that sometimes can cause confusion, especially if you are not used to so many available choices from the game's menu. It simply means that you can choose to play this game for a variety of per-line credits. For example, if you want to play for 1-penny per line, you would touch the on-screen icon that says: 1-cent. If you choose to play 10 lines at 1-cent per line, you are therefore wagering a total of 10-cents. Of course, on multi-denominational machines, you can also select different values. The most common choices are: 1-cent, 2-cent, 5-cent, 10-cent, 25-cent and $1 selections. The total value of each bet you make, therefore, increases as you select the higher denominations. If you are wagering 2-cent credits over 10 lines, your total wager is now 20-cents per bet. And so on, for each such selection. The beauty of this is that it gives you the choice of how much you want to spend on each wager and each line. On such machines and games you choose not only how many lines to play, but also the value of each credit. So, if you see a machine with more than one choice of denomination, this is what is meant by multi-denomination. "More than one choice in the value of the credits" is the easiest way to remember it.

As you can see, there is quite a lot to learn about all of these games, their configurations, and the various features and bonuses they offer. All of this information is valuable because it shows you how these games work, how they play, what features are available, what these features do, and how much they cost—before you actually go to the casino and use your own money to play them.

In the next chapter I will give you a short history of how these games evolved and how Aristocrat developed the new video slots that have "taken over the world." It is a very interesting story, and I hope you enjoy reading it. After that I will describe the specific games, adding as many photographs as possible to show you all of the steps you will encounter when you play these games. I will also explain what they are, what they do, and how they affect your entertainment experience and winning potential.

History Of Modern Video Slots

In this chapter I will focus on how one small Australian company revolutionized the world of modern casino slot machines with a new type of video slots now known worldwide as "Australian-style" slot machines. It is a very interesting story that will allow you an insight into how and why your favorite casino—and all of the casinos of the 21st century—have benefited from these innovations, and how and why they have come to be.

In the beginning...the 1950s

In 1951, Joe Heywood, a highly creative engineer and accomplished artist, began working with the Ainsworth Dental Company under the general management of the proprietor's son, Len Ainsworth. With a keen interest in gaming products, Joe realized that the Ainsworth Dental Company owned the equipment and facilities necessary to build a prototype gaming machine. He quickly focused Len Ainsworth's attention on the potential of such a project, and began to assemble the first working prototypes of a three-reel mechanical gaming machine.

By late 1953, production of the first machines, marketed as the *Clubman*™, commenced—initially, at the rate of two machines a week. The *Clubman*™ took the market by storm, largely due to the extraordinary engineering talents of Joe Heywood. Soon enough, machines were being built at a rate of four, and then eight, a week.

1 - Early Aristocrat slot machines, from the 1950s

Joe Heywood continually improved on his original designs. He launched a new timing clock (the mechanism responsible for reel speed) that was guaranteed for five years, ten times longer than the previous models. This revolutionary part was christened the Five Year Clock and launched with the first Aristocrat brand ma-

chine in 1953. It was also the first machine to be equipped with a *"cyclomatic bonus,"* an early progressive bonusing feature.

By the end of 1954, the business was producing twenty machines a week in a choice of one-sixpence or one-shilling de-nominations, and fast developing a reputa-tion for quality and durability, with ground-breaking mechanisms. In 1955, the company launched the *Club Master*™, a product larger than the *Clubman*™. It featured a number of

2 - Early Aristocrat *Cyclomatic* bonus machines

improvements including a distinctive eye-catching two-tone cabi-net, a self-sealing cash box and cash box door, and a mechanism permitting Multi Line and scattered payouts.

The innovations kept on coming. In 1959, the *Aristocrat Sheerline*™ was released, the only gaming machine with an all steel cabinet, full-width tray, score card, and lit reels. The first gaming machines with lights installed in Sydney were 24 Aristocrat *Gold Award*™ machines with Perspex fronts. They caused a sensation. The *Gold Award*™ machine offered, for the first time, two jack-pots—a single and a double. The 1950s proved critical in terms of establishing Aristocrat's reputation as a manufacturer of high quality, innovative and immensely popular gaming machines.

On the up and up...the 1960s

During the 1960s and most of the 1970s, Nevada was the only state in America where casino gambling was legal (and had been since 1931). Visits to Nevada in the late 1950s and early 1960s stimulated a number of ideas. Largely as a result of these visits, and some inspired design work by Joe Heywood, the ingenious *Aristocrat Nevada*™ machine was developed and launched to New South Wales, Australia in 1961. The first machine with a chrome door, it also contained a visible rotary throat (or rotary coin turret) that showed the last six to eight tokens inserted into the machine, thereby deterring the use of counterfeit coins. It was also the first machine that could display a prominent theme through a large illuminated area on the front. The *Aristocrat Nevada*™ was an enormous success.

3 - The *Club Master*™ and *Nevada*™ slots

Many themes developed during the early sixties were relaunched in later years, proving the strength of the early concepts that included *Inca Gold*™ and *Aztec Gold*™. Much of the original artwork was also designed by Joe Heywood.

Meanwhile, the company was opening up export opportunities. By 1961, Aristocrat was exporting 200 machines a week to

England on a Boeing 707. Two years later, in 1963, the Aristocrat *Grosvenor*™ came to be, offering the first automatic hopper payout with solid-state circuitry. It was the first console machine, the first with a conveyor cash collection unit, and the first with a verification meter (an anti-theft measure). Aristocrat then went on to launch its first machine in the United States in 1964, just prior to opening its first overseas sales office in Reno, Nevada. Their flagship gaming machine was entitled *Moon Money*™. In 1965, the *Aristocrat Mayfair*™ was released, the first solid-state electronically controlled machine, and the first with plastic reels.

Many more "firsts"...the 1970s

In 1972, the *Aristocrat 500*™ series was taken to market. It was the Australian debut of the mechanical "hold and draw" feature, permitting the player to "hold" two symbols and re-spin the remaining two reels. It was also the first machine with a "multiplier" feature allowing players to multiply the potential jackpot by the number of coins wagered on a line. The *Aristocrat 500*™ also included a progressive payout feature.

4 - The Aristocrat *500*™ series slots from the 1970s

Two further platforms were launched during the 1970s—the *Aristocrat Elite*™ in 1976 and the *Aristocrat Espri*™ in 1979. Together, they contained further revolutions in gaming technology: they were the first to provide both a single action kick-and-stop and single symbol reading mechanisms, and the first five-reel machines with a microprocessor, electronic credit meter, wide reels, and photo-optic binary decoding for payouts. Aristocrat had effectively put an end to mechanical gaming.

Here comes video…the 1980s

The 1980s saw Aristocrat acquire the leading market share in Australia and gain momentum farther afield, an example of which was the success of the *Aristocrat Elite*™ in Nevada. The first platform for this decade, the *Aristocrat Élan*™, was released in 1983. It was the first machine equipped with a coin carousel, drastically reducing the need for refills. Hot on its heels came the "world's largest" gaming machine, the *Aristocrat Matilda*™. This machine of mammoth proportions was handmade and extremely popular in New South Wales clubs. The *Aristocrat Microstar*™ machines were developed in 1984.

5 - Aristocrat's gigantic *Matilda*™

1987 proved to be a significant year for the company. Aristocrat introduced the first spinning reel video machine, the *Aristocrat Microstar II*™ machine (the MK II) and the *Goldstar*™ spinning reel video series. The first Aristocrat spinning reel video machines (MK IIs) were installed in Sydney, and had been designed to reflect the look and feel of two of Aristocrat's most popular mechanical spinning reel games, *Two Up*™ and *Inca Chief*™ They were extraordinarily successful. Performances on the machines virtually doubled as soon as they were installed, marking the birth of a new era of video gaming in which Aristocrat was to play a leading role.

Going public…the 1990s

The 1990s was a decade of lightning-quick technology. Aristocrat launched three separate product platforms, beginning in 1991 with *MK 2.5*™ upon the *500*™ series machines that fea-

6 - The first Multi Line video slot machine, as we know them today

tured a Multi Line multiplier. In 1993, the company put out the *540*™ series, the first nine-line video game.

Shortly thereafter, the *Mark IV*™ platform was unveiled, a graphically enhanced version of the 540 series that propelled the category's success to even greater heights. In August 1995, the *Mark V*™ platform was delivered, bearing a signature Aristocrat gaming concept, *Hyperlink*®, an advanced jackpot system. The debut *Hyperlink*® theme, *Born to be Wild*™, was placed in Queensland, Australia, and since *Hyperlink*® products similar to it have spread in popularity to the rest of the world. But perhaps the most significant turning point for Aristocrat came on July 9, 1996, when the privately owned business floated to the Australian stock exchange. Shares worth AUS $39.27 million were offered to the public at AUS $2.90 each, and Aristocrat Leisure Limited was born.

The 1990s was a decade of pivotal international growth for the company, with South African operations commencing shortly after the public float. In 1998, approval was granted for a full membership of the Japan Association of Electronic Amusement Machine Manufacturers. Aristocrat could now participate in two emerging and culturally specific jurisdictions. Trade in these markets would signal a departure from the company norm and the cultural diversification of Aristocrat's product portfolio.

Millennium…Year 2000 and up to the present

On August 24, 2000, the Nevada Gaming Control Commission approved Aristocrat's application for a license to manufacture. In 2001, the *MKVI*™ platform was launched in New South Wales within Aristocrat's new *XCite*™ cabinet and the *MKVI*™ platform was released in the USA in the *MAV*™ cabinet. That same year, Japanese players were introduced to the very first Aristocrat Pachislot game, *Triple Shooter*™, just as Aristocrat was completing a strategic acquisition of US systems company Casino Data Systems (CDS). CDS provided Aristocrat with a ready-made systems business, including infrastructure, staff, and the leading installed base of casino management systems. The extensive placement of their primary product, *OASIS*™, today branded as *OASIS 360*™, is to this day responsible for the company's U.S. systems business having the highest numbers of Class III casino customers of all manufacturers.

By 2002, Aristocrat's American head office had relocated from Reno to the hub of the American gaming industry—Las Vegas, Nevada. In 2003, the one-time family operative celebrated 50 years of trade, simultaneously enjoying landmark success in Australia with the first of their 50 Line products, *50 Lions*®. Japan went on to record a bumper year of financial results, effectively doubling their previous regional profit. By 2004, the Australian market had become relatively mature, causing the organization to shift expectations of growth offshore. The Americas subsequently recorded their best results to date from strong sales of *MKVI*™ product, in particular, *Millioni$er*®, the continent's first penny progressive slot machine with US $1 million top jackpot. A little closer to home, Aristocrat's floor share in the Sands Casino Macau doubled to almost 50% from the strength of standalone and linked products.

Back in Australia, more sophisticated products had been developed in an effort to increase value for customers in its mature markets. *Zorro*®, Aristocrat's original *Double Standalone Progressive*, a then highly advanced gaming concept, stands as one of the company's most successful products of all time. In 2005, offices opened in both Macau and Russia to better cater to the industry's newest emerging regions. Aristocrat set foot in the increasingly popular multi-station gaming product category by acquiring 50% of Slovenian company, Elektroncek, and partial acquisition of PokerTek Inc, an American manufacturer of the *PokerPro*™ electronic poker table. Aristocrat's European subsidiary also established an exclusive distribution partnership with company Aurora, an entity of a Russian market leader, SmartGames, for the Federation of Russia.

From the 1950s to the new millennium and beyond, Aristocrat has come a long way, yet maintains the spirit of adventure upon which it was founded more than half a century ago. Aristocrat currently supplies a wide portfolio of gaming products and services to more than 200 worldwide jurisdictions and has multiple offices in nine different countries. The company continues to be propelled by a momentum generated by unique gaming concepts, creative talent, and sharp business acumen. Whichever direction the industry may take, Aristocrat is committed to delivering entertaining games for players around the world.

And these, my friends, are just some of the reasons why I have chosen Aristocrat's games to showcase in this book. Aristocrat continues to produce leading-edge slot games and reel steppers, progressives, and Multi-Link systems for all the major casinos of the United States, as well as the rest of the world. And with that, let the games begin!

3

Bonus Features

There are many different kinds of features on modern slots, some of which are also called bonuses. All of them together are generally referred to as "game features," meaning they offer something more than the base game itself. The simplest ones are the free game features, but there are many others. These are either included individually in the game you have chosen to play, or a combination of them available in a variety of options. To help you understand exactly what these bonuses and features mean, here is a list of what people in the gaming industry call "game features."

Free Games

This is the simplest concept of all. Everything we now know as "game features" and "bonuses" grew and evolved from this basic idea. On most machines, free games are triggered by a combination of scattered symbols. A typical example of a free game feature is triggered by 3, 4 or 5 scattered symbols. These special symbols can appear anywhere on the game screen, and when they do they trigger traditionally anywhere from 8, 10, 15, 20 or 25—or more—free games. On many such games, while you are in the free games bonus, all the wins you achieve will be doubled or tripled—or enhanced with other bonusing features particular to that game. Great examples of precisely these kinds of games are *Adonis*®, and *Dolphin Treasure*®.

Free Games With Multipliers

The concept of free games quickly evolved into games that not only offered free games as a particular bonus, but also the additional availability of a multiplier bet for all wins achieved while within the free games feature. A "multiplier" is simply a numerical value—such as 2x, 3x, 4x, and so on—which then proportionately increases any of your wins while within that particular feature. For example, if you have a multiplier of 2x and your bonus win would have been 100 credits, you will now instead get 200 credits for the same win. In some cases you can multiply the win further by hitting specified combinations. For example, when you hit the substitute symbol on reels 2 and 4, this then allows an additional multiplier of 3x or 5x for that win. A great example of this is the game *Timber Wolf*™.

Bonus Games

First came the free game features. Then came the free game features with multipliers. The next evolution was "bonus games." Within the gaming industry the term "bonus games" is often used to describe modern games that include the use of an "ante" bet, also often referred to as a "bonus bet" because it requires players to wager additional credits in order to unlock an entirely new series of game features and bonuses. This can mean better payback for the entire game. As I mentioned earlier, an ante bet is similar to a "side bet" in table games like Let It Ride or Fortune Pai Gow.

Of course, you don't have to make such an additional wager. That is entirely your own choice. Similarly, you don't have to wager more than one credit per payline, or wager all of the available paylines. Games that offer additional wagering and winning opportunities in no way force you to participate in them, or use them. As in all forms of casino gaming, the choice of playing—as well as the amount you choose to wager and the features you choose to purchase—are up to you. I mention all of this again to make sure that everyone reading this book understands that I am writing about *available options* that adults participating in casino gaming have at their disposal. There are many choices, and part of the reason for writing this book is to show you what they are, and to advise you how to choose among them.

Two of the great games that are part of this "ante bet" or "bonus bet" family are the very popular *Mr. Cashman*®, and the more recent *Cashman Tonight*®.

Mixed Scatter Features

The next advancement in bonusing was the introduction of what are called "mixed scatters." For example, in the game *Sun & Moon*® you can win 10, 15 or 20 free games whenever 2, 3, 4 or 5 scattered "*Sun & Moon*®" symbols appear anywhere in the window. The reason these are called "mixed scatters" is that you don't have to hit only the "Sun" symbols, or only the "Moon" symbols. You can hit any combination of them—"mixed." These symbols have to appear left to right on active reels and lines. Once you are awarded them—and therefore receive the specified number of free games—all such wins during this feature are doubled. Both the *Sun & Moon*® standard, and *Sun & Moon*® *Double Standalone Progressive* (DSAP), utilize this mixed scatters feature. This is one of the simplest, yet one of the most exciting bonuses available. They happen very frequently, giving you not only great entertainment, but also anticipation combined with some very good wins.

Second Screen Features

The next evolution of the bonusing methodology is known as "second screen bonus features." Basically, whenever you hit the specified and required combination of symbols—be it scatters or some others (as displayed on the machine's pay screen)—the game takes you to another, and different, screen. The original screen is replaced by a new screen displaying the additional second screen bonus game and relevant features. The second screen bonus features can be anything, and can contain many different varieties.

The best way to find out what they are is to look at the machine's on-screen pay table, as well as the "Help" menu. This will show you if the machine you are about to play has such a second screen bonus, or perhaps even a third. It will also tell you what combination of symbols you must achieve in order to unlock such second or third screen bonuses. It will also explain how the second screen bonus works, how long it will last, and what you have to do in order to win something. In many such games, a second screen bonus will involve selecting something from the available choices that the second screen bonus will display for you. There are so many different varieties of second screen and third screen bonus features available, that it is virtually impossible to list them all. I advise you to look at the machine; all that information is available directly from the menu choices of the machine itself.

Classic examples of this kind of game are: *Where's the Gold*®, and the newer games *Party in Rio*™ and *Bonanza Bros.*™. I will describe these games later in the book.

Stacked Symbols

The next advance in bonusing is the use of "stacked" symbols. These are often "wild," but do not have to be. Basically, a "stacked symbol" simply means a series of the same symbol one on top of each other, often extending over the entire vertical reel on the machine. The principle is simple to understand, because once you see all of the same symbol stacked one on top of each other, filling the entire reel of the screen from top to bottom, you will know that this often means multiple winners over multiple lines or reels.

Great examples of these stacked symbol games are *50 Lions*® and its companion game *100 Lions*™, as well as the new game *Heart of Vegas*®.

Sticky Wild® Symbols

Another new bonusing feature is the concept of *Sticky Wild*® symbols. When we talk about "wild" symbols we usually refer to a symbol that replaces all other symbols. This means that whenever such a "wild" symbol appears, it will substitute and pay as if it were one of the other designated symbols for which it is "wild." For example, if such a wild symbol substitutes for, say, the picture of a cherry, and you need 3 cherries in order to win something, and you line up only 2 cherries on the payline—plus a "wild" symbol—then you are in effect winning the equivalent of hitting the 3 cherries. Of course, this is just an example, but the method applies equally well to any symbols, no matter what they are, and any such "wilds" however they may be designated on the machine you have selected to play.

But the concept of *Sticky Wild*® symbols is a new one, and it simply means that whenever such a wild appears in the free games feature—it will "stick" on the screen and remain there for the duration of the free games, while the rest of the reels spin around it. This means that you have more chances to get more wins, and bigger wins, especially as you "stick" wilds on the screen during such bonus features. Great examples of exactly this kind of a game are the venerable *Miss Kitty*® and *Pelican Pete*®, and also some of the newer games such as *Kick'n Ass*®. I will talk more about these games later in this book.

Risk vs. Reward

Another new concept in bonusing is to allow you—the player—to choose your own level of risk. On certain games you have the option of continuing with the bonus round—but at your own risk. What this means is that by that stage of the bonus round you have won a specified number of the cumulative credits—for example 2,500 credits as your bonus win. Now, instead of the bonus round being over, the game gives you the choice of continuing with the bonus round for bigger wins—but at an increased level of risk. If you choose correctly, you can increase the value of the wins exponentially. However, if you choose incorrectly, this choice now costs you some of the credits you had originally won. Most of the time such a loss value is about 50% of that win. Using the example of 2,500 credits as your initial bonus win, if you had chosen to continue the bonus round—at your own risk—and were unfortunate enough to make the fatal selection that ended the bonus round, your original win would have been reduced by 50%—meaning that you have now won 1,250 credits instead of the originally won 2,500. This, therefore, is the concept of "risk versus reward."

Naturally, you also have the opportunity to make the correct choices in continuing the bonus round, in which case you will increase your wins accordingly. On many of these games you can win several times more than the amount of your original bonus round win. To continue the example, if you chose correctly and continue through the bonus rounds successfully, your original 2,500 credits win could grow to 5,000 credits, or even more. All of this is clearly explained on the machine itself, in the paytable and bonus round screens. One of the best examples of exactly this kind of a game is the new machine called *Chicken2*™. I will tell you more about this entertaining game later in the book.

Choose Your Own Volatility

Anyone who has ever played a slot machine knows, at least intuitively, what the principle of "volatility" means. In simple terms, "volatility" is the frequency with which the game hits a pay, and the value of such a pay. High volatility games will not pay as often, but when they do pay, the pays are quite large. On the other hand, low volatility machines are those that pay frequently, but do not necessarily pay very much. Medium volatility games will pay prizes on average more frequently than high volatility games but the prizes will be larger than those in low volatility games.

Aristocrat has introduced new games that allow you—the player—to choose the level of volatility that you want to play, using the free game features. You can choose a higher number of free games, such as 25, but with a lower multiplier of, say 2x, or instead choose a lower number of free games, such as only 5, but with a high multiplier, say 10x. Personally, I prefer a high volatility game feature, because I play to win big prizes. I would almost always choose the high volatility feature in the game—but not always (I have more to say about this later on, but you'll have to read carefully to find out where I have placed the most valuable clue to this selection process.)

Just because I choose to play this way doesn't mean that this is the only way of doing it. It simply means that this is my general preference. Other players may prefer the low volatility game features, because they might want to spend more time enjoying the feature and the wins that it provides. Other players may prefer the medium volatility games, because they give you both a pay relatively frequently, as well as a higher value pay when you do get one. The best examples of these kinds of games are *5 Dragons*®, and the new *Cajun Magic*™.

It is, therefore, now time to get to the games....

4

Multi Line Games

What exactly are Multi Line games? Should I always play all the lines? Do I get fewer wins and bonuses when I play fewer lines? These are very good questions, and they are probably the most common ones that have been asked for as long as such games have been around. As I mentioned in Chapter 1, Multi Line simply means "more than one pay-line." Once you choose a Multi Line game, you immediately know this by the choices in the number of lines you can select to play. For example, many games have 20 lines, such as *Sun & Moon*®. You can, of course, choose to play just one payline, but that defeats the purpose of playing a Multi Line game in the first place. One of the attractions of playing Multi Line games is precisely that you can play more than one line. On a typical 20-line game you can choose 1-line, 5-lines, 10-lines, 15-lines, all the way up to the maximum available lines, in this case 20-lines.

One of the advantages of playing Multi Line games is that you can expand the field of accessible wins. Instead of having to rely on wins lining up on just one payline, as is common with the reel games, such as the ones with the spinning barrels and the handle to pull (called "steppers" in the industry), on Multi Line games for each extra line that you play you increase your opportunity to capture more wins, and even multiple wins on more than one payline. This has the direct effect of decreasing the volatility of the game, because now you have more of a chance to hit at least some kind of a pay much more often than is traditionally the case on machines with only one payline. Since this same concept applies to any game that has more than one payline, all such games are called "Multi Line" games.

Naturally, the more paylines that you activate, the more it will cost you to play the game. This also means that you will have a higher minimum bet, especially if you choose to activate all the paylines. In addition to multiple paylines, Multi Line slots also offer you the chance to wager more than one credit for each of your activated paylines. On most machines you will be able to wager anywhere from 1 to 10 credits, and on some machines even 25 credits or more. You can also select the value of each credit, particularly on what are called "multi denomination" games. Chapter 1 of this book explained what is meant by "multi denominational," which simply means that you have a choice of assigning the value of each credit. So, for penny games you can select the denominational choice of 1-cent equal to 1-credit, and so on for any value you choose to assign by selecting the appropriate denominational choice. Such machines and games allow you to play more than one payline, and to increase the wagers on each active payline. This not only spreads the field of potential wins by increasing the number of paylines, but also increases the value of each win, depending on the number of credits you have chosen to wager and the lines played.

For example, if you choose to play 20 lines at the value of 1-cent per line, then your total wager is 20-cents. But if the machine you are playing has multi-denominational choices and availability, you can also select from other values for each credit—such as perhaps 2-cent, 5-cent, 10-cent, or even 25-cents per credit, and on some machines even more. To use the example above, if you select 2-cent credit values and play all 20 lines, your total wager would now be 40-cents. Each time you increase the value of the denomination, the total wager will be higher. The same also applies if you choose to play more than one credit for each available activated payline. To continue with the same example, if you played the 1-cent value per credit over 20 lines, but chose to bet 2-credits per payline, then your total wager would again be 40-credits. Similarly, if the machine you are playing has a maximum of 10-credits per active payline, and you chose to play all the 20 lines available on a machine such as *Sun & Moon*®, then you will be wagering 20 x 10 credits as maximum wager. Therefore, your total wager will be $2.

As you can see, the benefits of playing Multi Line slots, as well as those that offer multi-denomination choices, places control over your gaming squarely in your own hands. You can bet as much, or as little, as is comfortable for you. Naturally, the more lines you play, and the more credits you wager, the more winning potential and possibilities you will receive, and the higher your wins will be. All of this is relative precisely to how you want to play, and what your purposes are in playing the game. If you're like me, and you like to get the biggest win possible, then you will always wager maximum credits over maximum number of lines. Naturally, this will require a much bigger bankroll than if you were simply playing the minimum of 1-credit per payline.

As a general rule, I advise you that for all the games I mention in this book, always play *at least* 1-credit over *all available paylines*. This is the best way to play these Multi Line video slots, as it gives you more ways to win. Here are some examples of Aristocrat's very successful Multi Line games:

Sun & Moon®

Now that you know what kind of Multi Line games are available on modern slots, and what they mean and how they work, I will show you some examples of great Multi Line games. Let's

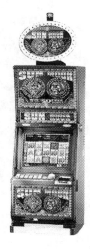

begin with *Sun & Moon*®, which in the Aristocrat family of slots is the catalyst for the explosion of modern machines in the United States and elsewhere in the world. The success of this game not only propelled the Aristocrat company into the American and world markets, but more specifically created the phenomenon now called the "Australian-style" game design.

7 - The classic and great *Sun & Moon*® video slot machine from Aristocrat

How the Game Plays

The game is available as a 20-line game and a 9-line game. It is usually found in low to mid denomination ranges. It is an average volatility game with a hit rate of about 15, which means that you will get a pay about every 15 spins. The game offers a bonus feature where you can win up to 50 free games with 2 or more scattered

8 - This is the *Sun & Moon*® main game screen.

GOLD or SILVER (of a kind, or mixed) symbols, occurring respectively from left to right. All wins during free games are doubled and the feature can be retriggered during the Free Games bonus.

Adonis®

Adonis is the handsome god of desire in Greek mythology. If you're interested in learning more about Adonis the Greek god, you can look him up on the Internet. But if you're interested in *Adonis*® the Aristocrat slot game, you have arrived at the right place. *Adonis*® is available as a 9-line game with a max bet of 45, 90 or 180 credits.

On this version you can also wager 5, 10 or up to 20 credits per payline. It is also available as a 20-line game, where the most likely max bet options are 100, 200 or 500 credits, and you can bet up to 5, 10 and 25 credits per line respectively.

The *Adonis*® symbol substitutes for all symbols, except scattered COIN symbols. As an additional bonus, all wins are doubled when the *Adonis*® symbol substitutes as part of a winning combination. The bonus rounds consist of 15 Free Games, which can be won with 3, 4 or 5 scattered COIN symbols. All prizes are tripled during the Free Games bonus, and the Free Games can be won again during the bonus feature. Whatever was the bet per line and lines played that you originally wagered will remain the same as that for the game that started the free games bonus feature. You can see this great game in Photo 9.

9 - The *Adonis*® video slot machine from Aristocrat

Dolphin Treasure®

In the aquatic world, fun-loving dolphins are man's best friend. Most people know them from Sea World, or some other aquatic entertainment park. They are also popular in movies and on television. I still fondly remember the TV show "Flipper," starring Brian Kelly in the role of Porter Hicks. The role of Flipper, the dolphin, was played by a female dolphin named Suzy, and occasionally by other dolphins Patty, Kathy, Scotty and Squirt—during the show's three-year run on television. The plots were silly and fun, the kind of fluffy family entertainment that was the staple of pure and innocent broadcasting on American television in the 50s and 60s.

10 - The *Dolphin Treasure*® video slot machine from Aristocrat

Dolphins are a universally recognized theme, and Aristocrat has several well-known and very popular dolphin-themed slot machines. *Dolphin Treasure*® is one of the original designs, featuring more of the innovative gaming technology and entertainment for which Aristocrat has now become world famous. The *Dolphin Treasure*® game is available as a 9-line and a 20-line Multi Line game and is mostly available to play in low and mid denomination. You can see this game in Photo 10.

Free Games Bonus

The bonus feature on *Dolphin Treasure*® consists of 15 Free Games, which are won whenever 3 or more scattered TREASURE CHEST symbols appear on the screen. During this bonus, all wins are tripled, and the Free Games bonus can be won again while in the bonus rounds.

11 - The *Dolphin Treasure*® main game screen, showing the winning of free games with 3 Treasure Chest symbols

12 - The great *Tiki Torch*® slot machine from Aristocrat

This is one of those great games that you will know instantly and want to play. It has been around for a few years and its popularity is still growing. It is a video slot game offered in 9- and 20-line versions, where all wins pay left to right on adjacent reels, including the scattered PEARL. The TIKI TORCH symbol substitutes for all symbols, except the scattered PEARL.

Tiki Torch® Free Games Bonus

One of the great attractions of this game is the Free Game PEARL Feature. It happens quite often, and every time it does you win 8 free games, along with any scatter wins. During the free games the KNIFE, CANOE and HOUSE symbols substitute for the TIKI TORCH. This means that you may see gigantic wins multiply across the screen as you rake in the credits. I have played this game many times, and each time it is just as much fun as it was before. I always find something fresh in it. The free games bonus feature can be won again during the free games, and the credits bet and lines played are the same as the game that started the bonus.

Bonanza Bros.™ is a new Aristocrat game, based on the popular *SEGA*™ video game. Today, many of the world's most popular

13 - The main game screen of the *Bonanza Bros.*™ video slot machine from Aristocrat

slot machine themes are created by the manufacturers. Aristocrat Technologies is at the forefront of leading game design, having created many proprietary titles that I mention in this book. *Bonanza Bros.*™, however, is a licensed theme that is popular worldwide. Aristocrat has taken this great video game and based a slot machine game around the popular characters created by *SEGA*™.

In this new slot machine game we have an excellent merger of concepts originally designed for video games, and those designed for slot machine games. Together, the *SEGA*™ video game and the Aristocrat *Bonanza Bros.*™ slot machine enhance the entertainment value for those already familiar with the game, and those who are familiar with slot machines. *Bonanza Bros.*™ spans the bridge between the video game and this slot machine. Everyone can enjoy this exciting new form of casino entertainment.

As with most machines, in this 25-line *Bonanza Bros.*™ game all wins begin with the leftmost reel and pay left to right on adjacent reels, except scatters. There are also several bonus rounds, as follows:

Free Games Bonus

In the Bonus Rounds, you can win between 3 and 10 free games with 1 to 3 WILD GOLD SYMBOLS. To get the bonus round you first must hit 3, 4 or 5 scattered SIREN symbols, which trigger the bonus free games feature. You will then move to a second screen feature and be prompted to touch a Character. The Character will start to collect DIAMONDS which represent the number of free games you will win. The symbols collected will become GOLD and wild during the free games, as follows:

- MEN symbols are replaced by GOLD MEN symbols
- CASH symbols are replaced by GOLD CASH symbols
- BAG symbols are replaced by GOLD BAG symbols
- PAINTING symbols are replaced by GOLD PAINTING symbols
- ACE symbols are replaced by GOLD ACE symbols
- KING symbols are replaced by GOLD KING symbols
- QUEEN symbols are replaced by GOLD QUEEN symbols
- JACK symbols are replaced by GOLD JACK symbols

All the GOLD SYMBOLS collected are now WILD and substitute for all other symbols—except the scattered SIREN symbols. The number of features remaining is indicated by the number next to the BAG. This bonus feature can also be triggered again while in the bonus rounds. The bet multiplier and number of lines played are the same as those you initially used to play the game at the time you hit the bonus feature.

In Irish folklore, if you find the leprechaun's pot of gold you can return it to him
and he will grant you three wishes. Not being
Irish, that's about the extent of my understanding of the folklore surrounding a leprechaun and
his pot of gold, but all of us have at one time or
another wished that we could find "where's the
gold," either a pot of gold, a gold field, a gold
strike, or in this case a slot game from Aristocrat.
This is a 25-line game, featuring DYNAMITE
symbols which are scatters. The scatter symbols
are also your entry into the bonus rounds. You
will need to achieve 3, 4 or 5 of these scattered
DYNAMITE symbols in order to unlock your
entry into the bonus feature, where you can win
anywhere from 3 to 10 free games and between
1 and 3 "Wild Gold Symbols."

14 - The *Where's
the Gold*® video
slot machine
from Aristocrat

Free Games Bonus

Once you have gained entry into the free games bonus feature, you will then be prompted to touch a character. Once you
have done this, a spotlight will shine on your selected character and
it will start mining. The number of free games you will win is equal
to the number of Gold Nuggets appearing in the window directly
below the spotlight. Any symbols appearing in this window are
replaced on the reels by GOLD SYMBOLS during the free games,
as follows:

- MINER symbols are replaced by GOLD MINER symbols
- MINE symbols are replaced by GOLD MINE symbols
- WAGON symbols are replaced by GOLD WAGON symbols
- PICK symbols are replaced by GOLD PICK symbols
- ACE symbols are replaced by GOLD ACE symbols
- KING symbols are replaced by GOLD KING symbols
- QUEEN symbols are replaced by GOLD QUEEN symbols
- JACK symbols are replaced by GOLD JACK symbols

In addition, all the GOLD SYMBOLS collected are now WILD, and substitute for all other symbols—except the scattered DYNAMITE symbols. The number of features remaining is indicated by the number next to the BAG. This bonus feature can also be triggered again while in the bonus rounds. The bet multiplier and the number of lines played are the same as those you initially used to play the game at the time you hit the bonus feature.

15 - *Where's the Gold®* game Bonus screen

You may be wondering why anybody would create a game called *Kick'n Ass®*. It's an excellent game, and the "Ass" referenced in the game's title is actually the animal kind, meaning a Donkey—and not the poker-playing kind either. This is a slot machine, and an excellent addition to the Aristocrat Multi Line family. It is a video slot game where all wins begin with leftmost reel and pay left to right on adjacent reels, including scattered HORSESHOE. Only the highest win on each line is paid, but all wins on different lines are added, and the scattered HORSESHOE symbols pay left to right anywhere on adjacent reels. The ASS symbol substitutes for all symbols, except scatters. The ASS symbol appears on reels 2 and 4 only, and the HORSESHOE symbol appears on reels 1, 2 and 3 only. You can see this game in Photo 16.

17 - The *Kick'n Ass*® slot machine game screen

16 - The *Kick'n Ass*® slot machine from Aristocrat

Sticky Wild® Free Games Feature

The *Sticky Wild*® feature was mentioned earlier in this book, and this game uses that concept. You can win 8 free games with 3 HORSESHOE symbols appearing left to right. When the ASS symbol appears on reel 2, it may reveal a multiplier which is shown as a 2x ASS. When an ASS symbol appears on reel 4, it may reveal a multiplier shown as 3x ASS. Any wins with either 2x ASS or 3x ASS that substitutes in winning combinations are also multiplied by 2x or 3x respectively. Any win with both a 2x ASS and 3x ASS substituting is then multiplied by 6.

Any ASS symbol, 2x ASS or 3x ASS appearing during the free games will stay in the window at that position for the remainder of the free games—meaning it will "stick" in that position. That is why games such as this are called *Sticky Wild*® games.

The scattered HORSESHOE symbols landing beneath any ASS or 2x ASS *Sticky Wild*® symbols may also contribute to a scatter prize, as indicated by the alternating display of these symbols. This bonus feature can be triggered again during the bonus rounds, but only once, with an additional 4 free games awarded. Credits bet and lines played are the same as the game that triggered the feature.

18 - The *Kick'n Ass®* *Sticky Wild®* bonus screen, with 3 scattered Horseshoe symbols

    I have spent quite a bit of time traveling around the world; I have been almost everywhere, except Antarctica and the North Pole. The North Pole is where polar bears live. I have never seen one outside of a zoo, but I have seen many documentaries about polar bears and Arctic wildlife. Some people call me an adventurer, although I think they are probably referring to my escapades in Las Vegas casinos, rather than my world travels. Nevertheless, I am used to "roughing it"—although my definition of "roughing it" is a penthouse with only one butler. Well, at least in my dreams.

19 - The *Dollar Bear®* game from Aristocrat

    Dollar Bear® is a 5-line slot machine game and is considered a high denomination game, meaning that the game is mostly available in denominations of $1 and up. It also means that even with only 5-lines, at $1 per line the minimum bet is $5. In fact, such a bet is equivalent to 500 credits on a 1-cent game. It is, therefore, comparable to all the games in this chapter whose maximum bet values are often equivalent to the minimum bet value on this game. It is also lots of fun to play, especially if you're like me and enjoy playing for higher stakes that provide the opportunity to win larger prizes. You can see this game in Photo 19.

All wins begin from left to right and pay on adjacent reels, except the scatters. The BEAR symbol substitutes for all symbols, except the scatters. Additionally, you can also win the Iceberg Feature.

Iceberg Feature

In addition to the pays on the base game, any 2, 3, or 4 ICE symbols trigger either 2, 5 or 10 bonus feature games respectively. During the bonus feature all wins are paid as a "bonus scorecard." This means that scattered ICE symbols pay in any position, and the feature can be retriggered again during the bonus rounds. All lines and bet values per line are played during the bonus rounds for the same values as the game that originally triggered this bonus feature.

20 - The *Dollar Bear*® Iceberg Bonus screen

5

50 & 100 Multi Line Games

By now most of us have become familiar with the concept of Multi Line video games. This concept includes the 9-line games, 20-line games and 25-line games. In addition to these, a new line of a very popular series of Multi Line games have been introduced to your favorite casino. These are the 50-line and 100-line games, featuring additional wagering opportunities, and increased opportunities for multiple wins across many lines. Since in all of these games wins on all lines are added together—often alongside scatter bonuses and other features particular to that game—the more lines you have, the more choices you have, and therefore the more wins you may receive. While it is true that Multi Line games require higher wagers in order to activate all the paylines, and often higher total bets in order to take advantage of all the pays that the machines offer, it is nevertheless one of those gaming choices that gives you the most bang for your buck.

As an old-time Las Vegas gambler, I prefer to play games where I can gamble to win something significant. These new slots, in 50-line and 100-line configurations, offer precisely that—an opportunity to wager larger amounts of money in order to get the biggest possible wins.

But that doesn't mean you have to do it this way. Many of these games can be installed as a two-for-one, meaning that you can purchase 2 paylines for just 1 credit. So, instead of having to wager 100 credits to activate all 100 paylines, you have to wager only 50 credits because you get a two-for-one. The same often also applies to the 50-line games, where you only have to wager 25-credits total in order to get all 50 lines. Therefore, as you can clearly see, even these high number of lines in Multi Line games offer many more choices, including the possibility of increasing the number of lines you play without having to increase your base wager amount.

In order to give you the best possible entertainment and gaming experience, and value, these games provide you with a multitude of choices. There are, of course, many other games—such as the ones I profile throughout this book—that offer different options. The book is designed to give you the broadest overview of these great new casino slot games, so that you can have a very clear idea of what they are, and how to play them, before you go to the casino and use your own money.

Looking back, I wish I had something like this book when I first began to play slots. It probably would have saved me a lot of money. At that time there were no books on the subject, and the only way to learn anything was to go to the casino with my own money, put it in the machines, and learn from experience. That is one part of the history of Las Vegas, and of gambling in general, that I don't necessarily miss. I am writing this book so that you can take this journey with me as we discover the world of the great new casino slots for the 21st century.

50 Lions® is the game that started it all. It began the revolution of high number of line, video games, which has now been expanded to many great titles—as you will see in the games featured in this chapter. In this game all wins begin left to right and all pays are only on adjacent reels and on active paylines. The game is available both in the version where 1-credit buys 1-payline, as well as the other version (mentioned earlier) where 1-credit buys 2-paylines. Additionally, the DIAMOND symbol—which appears only on reels 2, 3, and 4—substitutes for all symbols, except PROTEA. You can see this game in Photo 21.

21 - The *50 Lions®* Multi Line video game from Aristocrat

Bonus Feature

Whenever you achieve the three scattered PROTEA symbols on reels 1, 2 and 3, you will win 10 free games. With every free game played, an extra wild DIAMOND symbol is added to reels 2, 3 and 4, and remains "stuck" over an existing symbol for the remaining free games. In the free games feature, you can also re-trigger the feature, but only for 5 more additional free games. The total bet and lines played during the free games feature are the same as the ones with which you initiated the bonus.

22 - The bonus feature screen for the *50 Lions®* Multi Line video game from Aristocrat

The folks at Aristocrat saw another opportunity after the success of *50 Lions®*, and they came up with a brand new 100 line game based on that concept, and—naturally—called it *100 Lions™*. In simple terms, even more lines means more chances to win. On

top of this there is an even more exciting free game feature where you can win 10 free games, and where the number of wild DIAMOND symbols increases after every free spin. An additional 5 free games can also be re-triggered during the feature. Suspense associated with the safari theme is fitting of this "wildly" exciting combination of 100 lines, free spins, and wild DIAMONDs. You can see this game in Photo 23.

23 - The *100 Lions*™ Multi Line video game from Aristocrat

24 - The 100 line *Heart of Vegas*® Multi Line video game from Aristocrat

Another 100 line game is the new *Heart of Vegas*®. As with its namesake, this game celebrates a city of glitz and glamour, where showgirls reign and sequins sparkle brighter than the desert sun. It could only be Las Vegas, and the city's magic comes to life in *Heart of Vegas*®. In this game you can win 10 free games whenever three scattered SIGN symbols appear, and you can also win an additional 5 free games during the bonus feature. The game is a lot of fun, with stacked wilds and stacked symbols offering many chances at frequent and great wins. You will spot *Heart of Vegas*® in either low denomination 1-credit buys 1-line or 1-credit buys 2-lines. The main game is shown in Photo 24 and the "bonus" screens in Photo 25.

 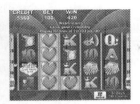

25 - The *Heart of Vegas*® stacked-wilds and bonus screens

A Purrrrr-fect Game!

Some people are dog people, and others are cat people. I have always been a cat person, although I have no problems with any of our four-legged friends. But cats are my thing … I just like them as pets, and basically anything with a feline motif—any item, or merchandise, with a "cat" theme. My best pet ever was a stray tabby cat that found its way to our back porch as a tiny kitten. We rescued it, and it was a valued part of our family for all the 14 years of its life. It was a wonderful cat, and a good friend.

So, whenever I find a slot machine with a "cat" theme, I investigate, and play. *Miss Kitty*® is a 50 Line video slot machine created by Aristocrat. It was first released in 2006, and since then has been a staple in most major casinos. It seems that there are many other people, like me, who like cats and cat-themed slots. You can see the game in Photo 26.

26 - The 50 line *Miss Kitty*® Multi Line video game from Aristocrat

Miss Kitty® can be found as a 50-line game in 1-credit buys one payline, or 1-credit buys 2-lines. In this second version, you get double the lines for what is essentially the same investment. One of the main attractions of *Miss Kitty®* is the CAT symbol (which is "wild") and animates when substituting for a win. During the free games the CAT symbol meows and the background tune plays with increasing tempo as more of the *Sticky Wild®* CATS are hit. There are also distinctive sounds for the *Sticky Wild®* CATS when you first hit them, and again when they substitute in a winning event.

Sticky Wild® Free Games Feature

27 -The *Miss Kitty Sticky Wild®* Feature screen

When 3 scattered MOON symbols appear, you will win 10 free games. Any CAT appearing during the bonus becomes a *Sticky Wild®* symbol, which means it stays in the window at that position for the remainder of the free games and substitutes for all symbols, except scatters. Any scattered MOON symbols occurring *beneath* the CAT symbols may additionally contribute to a scatter prize, as indicated by the alternating display of these symbols. This Bonus Feature can be triggered again during the bonus, but only once, with 5 free additional games won. Whatever number of credits you played at the beginning of the Bonus Feature—and lines played—will be the same for the bonus as well.

Pelican Pete® is a nautical-themed game. The graphics are appropriately populated with sea creatures, starfish, and even a treasure chest. There is a lighthouse with a prominent foghorn that sounds when you get three or more lighthouses. And, of course, the friendly pelican with a mouthful of coins. The LIGHTHOUSE symbol functions as a "scatter," and it animates with the bright arc light and the foghorn whenever it is won. The PELICAN symbol is "wild," and substitutes for all symbols (except scatters). It also animates when substituting in a winning combination. There are also many other sounds, with increasing tempo as more *Sticky Wild*® PELICAN symbols are spun up.

Sticky Wild® Free Games Feature

When 3 scattered LIGHTHOUSE symbols appear, you will win 10 free games. Any PELICAN symbol appearing during the free games stays in the window and substitutes for all symbols, except scatters. This bonus feature can be triggered again during the bonus rounds, but only once, with 5 more free games awarded. And when you do have a win, *Pelican Pete*® will open his beak with a mouth full of golden coins ready to fly to shore and bring you the bountiful gifts of treasure.

28 - The 50 line *Pelican Pete*® Multi Line video game from Aristocrat

Are you scared? Really scared? All in good fun, of course. If you're ready, then I dare you to open the creaking gate on *Jackpot Manor*™, the newest *GEN7*™ video slot title from Aristocrat. Ghosts, ravens, bats, and black cats roam the manor and the tomb-

stones out front. Trust me, this is one scary journey you will be glad you made. This new game is available as a 50-line game or a 100-line game in either 1-credit buys 1-line or 1-credit buys 2-lines configuration. Regular play is fun enough, but in *Jackpot Manor*™, there are twists and turns waiting with every spin.

29 - The 100 line *Jackpot Manor*™ Multi Line video game from Aristocrat.

Jackpot Manor™ Feature

First, three GATE symbols trigger the Feature of Fate! You then choose your fate by touching one of 20 Question Marks to reveal a credit value, a Key, or a Tombstone. If a credit value is revealed, you win that credit value. If a Key is revealed, you win the *Jackpot Manor*™ Free Game Feature. If a Tombstone is revealed, you win the Tombstone Bonus. So many wins! Yikes! Too scared to go on?

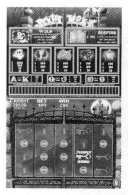

30 - The *Jackpot Manor*™ "Gate" bonus screen

Jackpot Manor™ Free Games Bonus

In the *Jackpot Manor*™ Free Game Feature, six free games are won. A glimmering candelabra displays the current multiplier for the free spins, and more free spins can be won during the feature. If three GATE symbols appear during the bonus, you move on to the Feature of Wealth. There, a selection screen will appear with 20 Question Marks. You are then asked to select one of the Question Marks to reveal the credit value you have just won.

31 - The *Jackpot Manor*™ Free Games bonus screens

Tombstone Bonus

In the Tombstone Bonus, a new selection screen will reveal 16 Tombstones.
Touch a Tombstone to reveal credits, a
multiplier, or a Key. Skull & Crossbones
are randomly buried and you are prompted to collect wins until one of the Skull &
Crossbones is revealed, at which point you
will win all of the accumulated credit values, multiplied by any multipliers found.
If the Key was found, the *Jackpot Manor*™
Free Games Feature will immediately follow the completion of the Tombstone Bonus. Multipliers apply to credits won in
the Tombstone Bonus only.

32 - The *Jackpot Manor*™
Tombstone Bonus screen

Frightening, isn't it? Or perhaps fabulously frighteningly great! Plan your next casino trip at Halloween, and see what great and ghoulish fun you will have with the *Jackpot Manor*™ game from Aristocrat.

I don't know how you feel about these cuddly creatures, but for me there is something inherently wonderful and innocent in that cute raccoon-like face and the overall gentleness of these extremely rare creatures. Pandas are world-renowned, and always prized wherever and whenever they can be found, including many zoos across the world. Being predisposed towards natural wonders, I tend to gravitate towards these kinds of themes. Make way for *Wild Panda*®, a 100-line video slot machine in the format of 1 credit for 2 lines. The game is generally installed in 1 and 2 cent denominations.

33 - The *Wild Panda*® slot machine from Aristocrat

Free Games Bonus

It is inevitable that creatures as cute as these will take you to a "wildly" exciting free spin feature in a game that is packed with mystical powers guaranteed to bring good fortune. Spell P-A-N-D-A on the five reels and you qualify for 5 free games. In the free spin feature all symbols involved in spelling P-A-N-D-A, and those particular symbols on all reels, turn into "Wild Panda" symbols. "Wild Panda" substitute for all symbols except the Coin. Take a thrill-ride with the *Wild Panda*® slot machine from Aristocrat.

Did you ever kiss a butterfly? This probably sounds like a strange question, considering we are speaking about a slot game, but in this case it refers to the gentle kiss that the sumptuous maiden in this game is going to send you, alongside—of course—beautiful wins. As with most games of this type, all wins begin with the leftmost reel and pay left to right on adjacent reels, except scatters. The GIRL symbols substitute for all symbols, except scatters. If one or more GIRL symbols substitute in a win, the pay for that win is doubled. When the GIRL symbol substitutes is a winning combination, the highest win is paid for that combination.

34 - The *Butterfly Kiss®* game from Aristocrat

Butterfly Bonus

The Free Games Feature is won with 3, 4, 5 or 6 BUTTER-FLY scatter symbols appearing anywhere on the screen. You then have a choice of selecting how many free games you want to play. The more free games you select, the lower the multiplier. However, the fewer free games you pick the higher the multiplier. Here are your choices:

- 20 Free Games - All wins multiplied by 2
- 15 Free Games - All wins multiplied by 3
- 10 Free Games - All wins multiplied by 5
- 5 Free Games - All wins multiplied by 10

The optimal strategy is to pick the middle two options, the ones with 15 and 10 free games respectively. This gives you the best chance for the most free games with a good value multiplier. Additionally, if the feature is triggered again while in the bonus round, with 4, 5 or 6 BUTTERFLY symbols where 2 of the BUTTERFLY symbols appear on reel 2, then the BUTTERFLY BONUS is won. The BUTTERFLY BONUS awards a prize between 20 and 4,000 credits.

6

Reel Power® Games

As I mentioned earlier, *Reel Power®* games are those where instead of buying paylines you are purchasing reels. The way this works is as follows:

- 1 credit buys ALL positions on Reel 1
- 3 credits buys ALL positions on Reels 1 & 2
- 7 credits buys ALL positions on Reels 1, 2, & 3
- 15 credits buys ALL positions on Reels 1, 2, 3, & 4
- 25 credits buys ALL positions on Reels 1, 2, 3, 4, & 5

By wagering the maximum credits—in this case 25-credits—you will purchase all positions on all reels. This is how you can achieve the 243 ways in which you can have a win. To help you understand this a little more easily, instead of having to "line up" on paylines, in these games the symbols just have to appear anywhere in the highlighted areas on adjacent reels from left to right. No paylines are needed.

There are many such games available in this configuration, with some also in the *Xtra Reel Power*™ versions. On these games you have in excess of 1,000 ways to win. I will show you the best of these games throughout this chapter. I begin with one of the most popular games available in casinos everywhere, called *Pompeii®*.

Pompeii® is now a slot game, but at one time it was a city in ancient Rome. Think of Pompeii as the San Francisco of the Roman era, with good living and a liberal attitude. With its sister city called Herculaneum, Pompeii was the retreat for Romans rich and famous—or infamous—all of whom came to the city at one time or another. Although everyone knew that it sat in the shadows of the great mountain called Vesuvius, which from time to time would belch and spew smoke and ash into the air, no one in ancient Rome paid much attention to it. It was a volcano, of course, one of the most active in the world. But human life spans in the ancient world were barely half that of ours today, and no one could remember the last time Vesuvius exploded. So life went on in relative peace and prosperity, pleasure and luxury.

And then came that fateful day in AD 79. On that day the Roman life in the ancient city of Pompeii went on as it had before, for all the years of the great Roman Empire. People went about their daily business, bakers baked their bread. Everyone in the city of Pompeii had seen the mountain belch with smoke and felt the rumblings of numerous small earthquakes over several weeks, but no one associated that with imminent danger. And then the great volcano erupted and buried both cities under many feet of ash.

Because of this tragedy, today we have perfectly preserved remains of life as it was in the ancient Roman Empire. The cities of Pompeii and Herculaneum have almost been entirely excavated, the streets, buildings, gardens, fountains, columns, frescoes, and even artwork are perfectly preserved.

The *Pompeii®* game is based on the majestic history of the city of Pompeii. The game pays left to right, where a VOLCANO symbol substitutes for all other symbols. To begin playing, you choose the number of reels you wish to play as well as the wager for each reel, and therefore the total number of credits you are going to bet on each spin. Your total bet is calculated as the number on the BET button multiplied by the number of credits on the REELS button. To open up the possibility and availability of all of the potential wins of which this game is capable it is advisable to play all reels.

35 - The *Pompeii®* slot machine from Aristocrat

Free Games Bonus

You can win 10, 15 or 20 free games when any 3, 4 or 5 scattered COIN symbols appear in a winning scatters combination. During the free games, any win with a VOLCANO symbol that substitutes anywhere on both reel 2 or 4 is then multiplied by 3 or 5 respectively. Any win with a VOLCANO symbol substituting anywhere on both Reel 2 and 4 is then multiplied by 15. The free games feature bonus can be won again during the bonus rounds. The reels selected and the bet multiplier during the bonus are the same as the game that started the feature.

There's a lot to be said for a party in Rio! Down in the city and at the Copacabana, below the guardianship of Sugarloaf Mountain and on the golden expanse of the sandy beaches at the

36 - The great *Party in Rio*™ slot machine from Aristocrat

half moon bay, all eyes point to Rio de Janeiro for party time! Some of the people of Rio de Janeiro seem to have the word "party" as part of their birthright; somehow they seem to be born with the inherent ability to "party all the time." There is much to be said for this lifestyle, of course, and for almost 25 years my life in Las Vegas has been very much like that. But every party-goer eventually needs sleep, so these days I tend to confine my party time to slot machines, such as this *Party in Rio*™ game from Aristocrat.

This is a *Reel Power*® game where all wins begin with the leftmost reel and pay left to right on adjacent reels, except scatters. The GIRL symbol substitutes for all symbols, except scatters. The GIRL symbols appear only on reels 2, 3 and 4.

Bonus Features

There are two terrific bonuses in the *Party in Rio*™ game, where you can win up to 20 Free Games. The first is the Samba Free Games Bonus, and the second is the Rio Girl Bonus which occurs during the free games.

Samba Free Games Bonus

You can win this bonus with any 3 or more scattered WHISTLE symbols. A selection screen appears with 10 musical instruments. As you select 5 instruments, the sound of that instrument plays and reveals the number of free games you have won. All wins, except bonus prizes, that are achieved during the free games are always doubled.

37 - The Samba bonus screens for the *Party in Rio*™ slot machine

Rio Girl Bonus

Each GIRL symbol appearing during the free games awards an extra BONUS prize of 1, 2, 5, 10 or 20 credits. This is in addition to the bonus wins that are already displayed on the screen, and which were multiplied by the total number of credits wagered. The bonus features can be triggered again during the bonus rounds. The bet per reel values and reels played are the same as the game that triggered the bonus.

5 Dragons®

5 Dragons is a *Reel Power®* game where all wins begin with the leftmost reel and pay left to right only on adjacent reels. You are first asked to choose your number of reels, and then choose your bet per reel to begin the game. The GREEN DRAGON symbol substitutes for all symbols, except the scattered COIN symbols. The GREEN DRAGON symbols appear on reels 2, 3 and 4 only. To trigger the

38 - The *5 Dragons®* slot machine from Aristocrat

free game feature the scattered COIN symbols need to appear left to right anywhere on adjacent reels.

39 - The *5 Dragons*® main game play screen

Free Games Bonus

There are 5 different choices in the Free Games Bonus. The free games are won with any 3 or more scattered COIN symbols, appearing on the screen from leftmost reel to right. A second screen will then appear displaying five feature options, which allows you to choose which feature you prefer. Your choices are as follows:

20 Free games - All wins with WHITE DRAGON substituting are multiplied by 2x, 3x or 5x

15 Free games - All wins with RED DRAGON substituting are multiplied by 3x, 5x or 8x

10 Free games - All wins with BLACK DRAGON substituting are multiplied by 5x, 8x or 10x

8 Free games - All wins with BLUE DRAGON substituting are multiplied by 8x, 10x or 15x

5 Free games - All wins with YELLOW DRAGON substituting are multiplied by 10x, 15x or 30x

During the free games the PACKET symbol appearing anywhere on Reels 1 and 5 results in a bonus prize of 2, 5, 10, 15, 20 or 50 additional credits, which are multiplied by total number of credits wagered. This Free Games Bonus can be won again during the free games. The reels selected and the bet multiplier during the feature are the same as those on the game that started the feature.

40 - The *5 Dragons*® Bonus screen

Is there a crazy chicken in your future? Or how about an ordinary chicken? No, not the kind you eat for dinner—I mean the kind you get on a slot machine. Confused? Well, don't be. *Chicken2*™ is a great *Reel Power®* game from Aristocrat. It offers you not only great pays and a terrific bonus, but also the opportunity to increase your bonus by taking just a little bit of a risk. However, you are not the one taking the risk—it's that crazy chicken!

This game just cracks me up! I have played many slot machines, and enjoyed all of the great games that I describe in this book, but if I had to pick a favorite, this crazy chicken would be it. Not just because of the incredibly funny graphics, or the fact that the game plays and pays very well, but because of the insane bonus when the chicken tries to cross the road and—if it's not *very* careful—gets splattered by a passing truck. You see, there's this chicken trying to cross the road. When it's very careful, the trucks go right past it, and it then gets to the other side and wins you some credits. But then it's not sure if it should cross again, and that's where you have to decide whether or not to make it go across the road. If it's not the right choice, wham! There goes the truck, and there goes the chicken, feathers flying everywhere. Even now, as I write about this game I can't help but laugh.

The *Chicken2*™ slot game gives you an opportunity to risk something in the bonus round in order to get a bigger bonus. The way this works is that after the chicken has two successful crossings, the Bonus is over; now you have to choose if you want to risk the chicken crossing the road again, in order to award you more bonuses. As long as the chicken successfully crosses the road, your bonuses continue to increase. But when the chicken gets splattered by the truck, well, that is the "risk." You see, if that happens you will lose half the bonus credits that you have accumulated up to this point. So, the bad news is that you lose half the credits if this happens, but the good news is that you still won some credits in the bonus, so it's really not all that devastating. That is the concept of risk vs. reward which is part of this particular game. This kind of a bonus structure is available on other Aristocrat games as well. Anytime you are playing a game that gives you an option of continuing the bonus past its normal termination time, this is a game where you can risk a portion of the credits you have won so far

in the bonus in order to receive a bigger bonus, or walk away with only half of that win if the bonus round ends unsuccessfully for your challenge.

Which now brings us to the age-old question: Why did the chicken cross the road? The common answer is: "Why, to get to the other side." Well, take a good look at that crazy chicken in Photo 41,

41 - The crazy chicken in *Chicken2*™, the brilliant game from Aristocrat

and you have the answer. It was the chicken itself that flew the coop! And with that, dear friends, I think it's time to explain a little bit more about this game, the bonus, and how it all plays and pays.

How to Play *Chicken2*™

In *Chicken2*™, all wins begin with the leftmost reel and pay left to right on adjacent reels, except scatters. Scatter DYNAMITE symbols pay in any position, and the EGG symbol substitutes for all other symbols, except scatters. The EGG symbol appears on reels 2 and 4 only. Any win with the EGG substituting on reel 2 only is multiplied by 2, and any win with the EGG symbol substituting on reel 4 only is multiplied by 2, 3, 4 or 5. Additionally, any win with the EGG symbol substituting on reels 2 and 4 at the same time is multiplied by 4, 6, 8 or 10. Each symbol can be used only once per winning combination. Only positions containing the winning symbol are used in determining the win for that symbol.

Dynamite Chicken Bonus

You can win this bonus feature with any 3 or more scattered DYNAMITE symbols. The chicken will automatically cross the road twice to get the prizes. The prizes that the chicken gets are added to the prizes-collected meter as indicated on the machine. You can then touch either the "CROSS AGAIN" symbol to continue the bonus, or the "LEAVE NOW" symbol to end the bonus. If you choose to leave, the prizes collected by the chicken so far are awarded to you. If you choose to continue by pressing the cross symbol, and the chicken crosses the road successfully, then another prize is added to the prizes-collected credit meter.

42 - The great *Chicken2*™ slot machine from Aristocrat

43 - The Dynamite Scatter symbol for the *Chicken2*™ game from Aristocrat

If you choose to cross, and the chicken is splattered by the truck, then half of the prizes collected are awarded (rounded up to the nearest credit), and the bonus feature ends. You can touch the cross symbol up to a maximum of 6 times. If you're successful all six times, you will be very happy collecting huge bonuses—and the crazy chicken will remain un-splattered.

And that, my friends, is the story of the chicken. I hope I won't meet any trucks next time I cross the road.

Timber Wolf™

A howling Wolf, a mist-covered moon, and a wise owl with a penetrating gaze, along with *Sticky Wild*® features and multiplier bonuses, all await you in this game. When you play *Xtra Reel Power*™ the game screen is in a 4 x 5 format and has 1,024 ways to win. It is a game where all wins begin with the leftmost reel and pay left to right only on adjacent reels, including scatters. The MOON symbols substitute for all other symbols, and appear on reels 2 and 4 only.

44 - The *Timber Wolf*™ slot machine from Aristocrat

Free Games Bonus

You can win 12 free games with any scattered OWL symbols win, from leftmost reel to right on adjacent reels. During the free games, if a MOON substitutes in a win on reel 2, that win will be multiplied by a factor of 3x. If the MOON symbol substitutes in a win on reel 4, that win will then be multiplied by a factor of 5x. If the MOON symbol substitutes in a win on reels 2 and 4 together, that win will then be multiplied by a factor of 15x. If the MOON symbol appears on reels 2 and/or 4 in a bought

45 - The *Timber Wolf*™ bonus screen

position and does NOT substitute in a win, then the reel(s) with the MOON symbol are held, and all other reels re-spun once. The free games bonus feature can be won again during the bonus rounds, but the re-spin cannot be won again during the re-spin itself. The reels selected and the bet per reel during the feature are the same as those on the game that started the feature.

Stampede of Wins!

There was a time, about 150 years ago, when giant herds of buffalo roamed across the plains which would eventually become the Dakotas and Indian territories, stretched from horizon to horizon and from the north to the south. Great swaths of land were covered by these gigantic herds numbering millions of buffalo. One of my favorite films of all time is "Dances with Wolves," set in the era just after the Civil War, and just before the demise of the great Sioux tribes of the Dakotas. There is a scene in the movie depicting the great buffalo hunt, where large areas of ground were turned brown by the hooves of the great herd. When more than 1,000 pounds of full-grown bull buffalo is charging at you full stride it can be an awesome sight indeed, even in a movie. Now you can experience that thrill in this new slot machine from Aristocrat.

46 - The *Buffalo*™ slot machine from Aristocrat

Buffalo™ is one of the new generations of *Reel Power®* slots from Aristocrat, this one in the *Xtra Reel Power*™ series. All wins begin with the left-most reel and pay left to right only on adjacent reels, except the scatters. The COIN symbols are the scatters, and they pay in any position. The SUNSET symbol substitutes for all symbols, except the scattered COINS, and appear on reels 2, 3 and 4 only. The other symbols on the game are: Buffalo, Eagle, Cougar, Wolf and Elk. The game is available in a range of denominations, from 1-cent credits and up and the max-bet options are 200 and 400 credits.

Free Games Bonus Feature

You can win 8, 15 or 20 free games when 3, 4 or 5 scattered COIN symbols respectively appear anywhere in the screen. During the free games each SUNSET symbol—which appears anywhere on reels 2, 3 or 4—will multiply the total win for that spin by either a factor of 2 or 3. The Bonus Feature can be won again during the bonus rounds.

47 - The free game bonus feature in *Buffalo*™ is triggered by 3 or more COIN symbols

In addition, 5 extra free games are awarded if any 2 scattered COIN symbols occur during any free game. The reels selected and the bet multiplier during the feature are the same as those on the game that started the feature.

7

Power Pay™ Games

*P*ower Pay™ is the "extra wager" or "ante bet" concept that allows you—the player—to wager additional credits in order to unlock more winning opportunities. It is one of those extra bet concepts, or a side bet, such as those with which you may be familiar from some table games. *Power Pay*™ games can be available in both Multi Line or *Reel Power*® machines. These *Power Pay*™ "ante bets" give the game designers more opportunities to add additional winning and bonusing options to the game, while at the same time giving players a chance to win more by having this additional choice. To find out if you are about to play a *Power Pay*™ game, look for the *Power Pay*™ logo on the screen or on the button panel. When you activate *Power Pay*™ on a *VIRIDIAN*™ game, the top screen on the machine will change, showing the different pays, bonuses, and all other applicable pays which are now activated. In most instances this also adds a better payback percentage to the game's overall payback. When you take all these features into account, you'll see that *Power Pay*™ games are some of the best choices available for your gaming entertainment.

    Power Pay™ is all about choice. If you are going to play a *Power Pay*™ game, then I would suggest that you play maximum credits to activate all the *Power Pay*™ features that the game offers. To do otherwise would be akin to playing a wide area progressive that requires maximum wagers, but choosing to play it for less. If you did this, and you did hit the progressive, you wouldn't be paid—because you failed to take advantage of the choice the game offered you, which was to wager the additional credits in order to be eligible for such a jackpot. The same principles apply to any "extra bet" or "ante bet" game.

Lucky 88® is one such *Power Pay*™ game. While you can play it without the extra bet, it is significantly to your advantage *not* to play that way, but instead to play the game *with* the full extra wager requirements. This will give you the biggest bang for your buck, as well as significantly higher pay values, more bonuses, and certainly a great deal more entertainment. Nevertheless, the game does offer you the choice of playing it with, or without, this extra bet. I think you will see very clearly that you get a lot more by playing the game with the extra bet. The simple base game without the extra wager is still a terrific game to play, and it does offer value and entertainment commensurate with the features that are offered on the game without utilizing the extra bet option.

In this chapter I profile several of the most popular and newest games in the *Power Pay*™ family, and provide information about how to play them, and show you their pictures. These games are representative of all the games in the *Power Pay*™ family. If you find a game in your favorite casino that is not featured in this chapter—but it is marked as a *Power Pay*™ game—you can approach it by following the same principles I include in this chapter. Let's begin with *Cajun Magic*™, one of the newest titles in the *Power Pay*™ family of casino slots.

There is something inherently wonderful about the Cajuns, not only because of the mystery surrounding Cajun country and its people, but also because of the cooking. I absolutely adore Cajun cooking, although I need to be standing near a fire truck in order to put out the blaze in my stomach when I eat it. But we don't have to worry about burning our belly with the *Cajun Magic™* slot machine. This great game from Aristocrat is a video slot machine where all wins begin and pay left to right, and where the FIREFLIES symbols substitute for all other symbols. These FIREFLIES symbols appear on reels 2 and 4 only. You can also win a free games bonus feature whenever you line up any 3 or more scattered

48 - The *Cajun Magic™* *Power Pay™* slot machine from Aristocrat

49 - The *Cajun Magic™* *Power Pay™* slot machine main game screen

TREE symbols left to right on adjacent reels and/or lines. When you play the *Power Pay™* feature you are awarded 5 additional bonuses when the free game feature is won.

Free Games Bonus Choices

As mentioned above, the free bonus games are won with any 3 or more left to right TREE symbols. The game then displays a second screen, where you are asked to choose the volatility of the free game feature, e.g. either a high number of games with lower substitute multipliers (in this example FIREFLIES), or a lower number

50 - The *Cajun Magic™* *Power Pay™* bonus game is won with 3 or more scattered TREE symbols.

of games with a higher substitute multiplier. And, if you played using the *Power Pay*™ button, you will also get an additional 5 free games.

POWER PAY™	NON POWER PAY™
Free games chosen	
25 FREE GAMES	20 FREE GAMES
20 FREE GAMES	15 FREE GAMES
15 FREE GAMES	10 FREE GAMES
13 FREE GAMES	8 FREE GAMES
10 FREE GAMES	5 FREE GAMES

Chart 1 - The number of Free Games that can be chosen in the *Cajun Magic*™ *Power Pay*™ slot machine from Aristocrat

If the GIRL symbol appears on reels 1 and 5, a bonus prize of 2, 3, 5, 10, 20 or 50 credits —multiplied by the total credits bet—is awarded. This bonus feature can be triggered again during the bonus rounds. Bet per reel and reels played are the same as the game that triggered the feature.

In Western culture the number 7 is considered lucky. That's why there are so many 7 symbols everywhere on our favorite games. But in Oriental culture it is the number 8 that has the "lucky" significance. A single 8 is considered *very* lucky, and the double 8 configured as 88 is considered *extremely* lucky. *Lucky 88*® is a game based on this concept, a brand-new *Power Pay*™ video slot machine whose game play and bonus features are all based in and around the number 8 and its various multiplication factors. If you've never experienced so many 8s on any game before, get ready for a truly exciting trip into the world of Oriental gaming.

In *Lucky 88*® all wins begin with leftmost reel and pay left to right only on adjacent reels, except for the scattered LANTERNS. All wins—except scatters—are multiplied by the amount of credits bet per line.

51- The *Lucky 88*® *Power Pay*™ slot machine from Aristocrat

Bonus Feature

The bonus feature is triggered with 3 or more scattered LANTERN symbols. Once you hit the feature, you will be offered a multitude of choices. If you are *not* playing the *Power Pay*™ ante bet, you will be prompted to choose one of the following:

- **20 free games**. During this bonus, if one or more MAN symbols substitutes in a win, then the pay for that win is multiplied by 5 or 18 times the win.

- **10 free games**. During this bonus, if one or more MAN symbols substitutes in a win, then the pay for that win is multiplied by 8 or 38.

- **3 free games**. During this bonus, if one or more MAN symbols substitutes in a win, then the pay for that win is multiplied by 18 or 88.

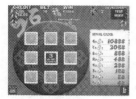

52 - The *Lucky 88®* *Power Pay*™ "Dice" bonus screen

If you *are* playing the *Power Pay*™ ante bet, once you trigger the feature you will be offered the above choices but with an additional 5 free games or the Dice Bonus. The Dice Bonus consists of 3 dice games. Each dice game starts with the 8 outer dice being rolled. If one or more number 8 is rolled, then all the 8s are held and the remaining outer dice are rolled again. This continues until no more 8s are rolled. At the end of each dice game a prize is awarded for the number of 8s rolled.

These prizes are multiplied by the bet per line on the game that triggered the feature, as shown on the screen. At the completion of any 3 dice games, the middle die is rolled again. If it displays the message "3 More Games," another 3 dice games are played. This bonus feature can be triggered again during the free games.

Just a little bit naughty, and so you are sure to fall victim to the allure of *Wicked Winnings II*™, the *Power Pay*™ video slot machine from Aristocrat. With a devilish theme, a riveting *Reel Power*® base game, and enchanting *Power Pay*™ bonus options, this game may seem like it's going to give you hell, but instead can give you the chance of heavenly profits. *Wicked Winnings II*™ features a different style of *Power Pay*™ game play. Rather than an additional 5 credit ante bet, *Wicked Winnings II*™ has a 25-credit ante bet which essentially doubles your bet, making it a 50c bet on a 1c game, 25c to cover all lines and 25c to play the ante bet. The unique *Power Pay*™ features of *Wicked Winnings II*™ include Free Games, Multipliers and Re-Spins.

Wicked Winnings II™ can be found as a 250 or 500 credit max bet and typically installed as a 1- and 2-cent denomination game, so look for it in the low denomination areas of your favorite casino. You can see what it looks like in Photo 53.

In this game, all wins begin with leftmost reel and pay left to right only on adjacent reels, except scatters. The WOMAN symbol substitutes for all other symbols, and appears on reels 2, 3 and 4 only. The Scattered MONEYBAG symbols pay in any position in the window across all lines and reels.

53 - The *Wicked Winnings II™* *Power Pay™* slot machine from Aristocrat

Power Pay™ Bonus Features

In order to be eligible for the bonuses, you must play the *Power Pay™* bonus wager. To do this, simply touch the *Power Pay™* button on the button deck. That will initiate the *Power Pay™* option. Among the bonus features offered are the following:

Re-Spin Feature

54 - The *Wicked Winnings II™* Re-Spin Feature game screen

Whenever 3 WOMAN symbols occur on the same reel, those reel(s) are held and the other reel(s) are re-spun once. This re-spins feature can be triggered again during the re-spin bonus rounds. The bet per reel and reels played are the same as the game that triggered the re-spins bonus.

Free Games Feature

Whenever a background FLAME symbol appears on both reels 1 and 5, you will win 15 free games. The free games can be triggered again during the Free Games Feature, as well as the re-spin feature. The re-spin feature can also be triggered again during the Free Games Feature. The bet per reel and reels played are the same as the game that triggered the Free Games Feature.

55 - The *Wicked Winnings II*™ *Power Pay*™ game screen, showing how free games are won when the burning symbols appear on reels 1 and 5

8

Multi Game Machines

Aristocrat brands their Multi Game products as *Player's World*™.
Multi Games are a package of games that combine a number of
new and proven Aristocrat titles. I mention several of these great games in this chapter, but for
purpose of clarification "Multi Games" simply
means a collection of games within the same
cabinet. You can identify a Multi Game when
you first approach the machine by looking at
the main game screen. If on the main game
screen you see choices of available games, such
as 2 games, or 4 games, or perhaps even more,
then this is a Multi Game machine. You can see
what it looks like in Photo 56.

    The Multi Game packs therefore give you
a choice of playing different games by simply
selecting them from the menu instead of having
to get up from the game you are playing and
find the next game you want to play in another
cabinet located elsewhere in the casino.

56 - The *Player's
World by Demand*™
Multi Game
machine from
Aristocrat

In a nutshell, this is gaming made simple. The more such choices the unit has, the less you need to walk around and hunt for the games you like to play, or search for new games you would like to experience. There are several such titles now available in the *Player's World*™ multi game package. I begin with a new game—*Players World by Demand*™.

As I said earlier in this book—and as I have been saying for many years—the world of casino gaming in the 21ˢᵗ century is all about choice. By that I mean *your* choice, not just the casino's choice, or the choices of the people who make the games. Not so long ago your choices were limited to either this machine, or this game, or another. Each time you wanted to change machines, or play for lower stakes—or perhaps higher stakes—you had to hunt around the casino not only to find the games you wanted to play, but also the right denomination, the number of lines you wanted to choose, and many other features that were predetermined by the manufacturer of the game, or the casino, or perhaps both. This meant a lot of walking, and believe me I know! In the 26 years I have been in Las Vegas I have walked across every casino floor in every casino—and not just in Las Vegas, but everywhere throughout the United States. That's a lot of walking!

Most of the time, I was doing this because I wanted to see all the available games and find the ones I wanted to play for my own personal enjoyment. This meant I had to go looking for those games as well as the configurations that I wanted, themes in which I was interested, and the money value I wanted to play for. These days it is very different, because games such as *Players World by Demand*™ offer a multitude of choices—choices that, prior to the introduction of this game concept, required all that walking. Now we can just sit in front of the game, and choose what we want to play from the menu, as well as the lines, the denominations, and the many other features that *Players World by Demand*™ now offers.

Imagine giving yourself even more opportunities to switch games, as well as to switch denominations whenever you want, without losing credits or even changing seats! Now you can put the ultimate power of choice in your own hands with *Players World by Demand*™, Aristocrat's first ever Multi Game and multi-denominational product package. This innovative new offering brings four of Aristocrat's best games together in one machine. Only *Players World by Demand*™ lets you choose one of three different denominations: 25c, 50c or $1. Plus, you can choose to play any one of four highly sought-after great games: *Big Red*®, *Black Panther*®, *King of Asia*® and *Super Bucks IV*™.

Players World by Demand™ lets you select your game and denomination on the main screen and gives you the option of changing games and denominations *whenever you wish* to do so. For you—the player—this is the ultimate in flexibility, control and, most importantly, fun.

57 - The *Player's World by Demand*™ multi-game menu choice screen

58 - The *Players World by Demand*™ 4-Pack gaming console from Aristocrat

One of the advantages of the *Players World by Demand*™ multi-game machine is that it provides higher denomination options than many other versions of these games. While it is true that you need a bigger bankroll to play these games at these values, it is also true that you have the chance to win greater wins. *Black Panther*® has no free game feature, but there are more base game wins.

Personally, I like to play higher denomination games because I enjoy the large jackpots that these games offer. The *Black Panther*® symbol substitutes for all symbols, providing increased opportunities for good wins—especially in these higher denominations.

In this Australian-themed game, you can win 5 free games for each played lighted line, where one or more KANGAROO symbols substitutes in a win. Each TREE symbol that appears during the 5 free games repeats the KANGAROO win that initially triggered the 5 free games. All free games are played on the 5 line version of the game.

In this *King of Asia*® Oriental-themed game, whenever 3 scatters appear on the reels, you will win 10 free games. With every free game played, an extra wild MAN symbol is added to reels 2, 3, 4 and 5 for the remaining free games. This free games feature can be triggered again while in the bonus round, but only once, and only with 5 more free games.

In *Super Bucks IV*®, the bonus feature is won with 3 or more scattered BADGE symbols. You are then asked to choose your free games feature by touching the color of your choice, as follows:

- The YELLOW choice wins you 10 FREE GAMES— where all wins are multiplied by 2
- The RED choice wins you 8 FREE GAMES—where all wins are multiplied by 3
- The BLUE choice wins you 6 FREE GAMES—where all wins are multiplied by 4
- The PINK choice wins you 4 FREE GAMES—where all wins are multiplied by 6
- The GREEN choice wins you 3 FREE GAMES—where all wins are multiplied by 8

During each of the free games 1, 2 and 3 extra free games are won whenever 1 or 2 (and no more than 2) scattered BADGE symbols appear anywhere in the window. In this game, in my opinion your best strategy choices are the "red" and the "blue" selections, because they give you the best number of free games with a decent multiplier.

As you can see, *Players World by Demand*™ offers not only the convenience of choosing a game from the menu on a single gaming console, but also the benefits of higher denominations that produce significantly bigger wins. If you consider these games as part of your overall gaming choices, then you have once again increased your range and breadth of available gaming entertainment, while at the same time gaining an opportunity to graduate your gaming as your wins increase. As any gambler knows, the trick to winning more is to parlay the wins. Now you have the opportunity to take the wins you may have scored elsewhere, and go to these games and give yourself the chance to multiply those wins exponentially by playing the higher denominations offered.

Give yourself the "Royale" treatment! *Jackpot Royale®* is the game named to the 2009 list of CEM Magazine's Top 10

Technology Award winners. It sets new standards in the slot world by presenting the first multi-game, multi-denominational capability *Double Standalone Progressive* jackpot.

What's really new and exciting about *Jackpot Royale®* is that the number of lines automatically changes depending on the denomination you choose. For example, if you choose a 5 cent denomination, the game automatically changes to 25 lines. If you choose a 10 cent denomination, the game automatically changes to 10 lines, and if you choose a 25 cent denomination it becomes a 5 line game. It is still the same game; it simply adjusts for the denomination selected and provides the appropriate per line and max bet options.

Jackpot Royale® has two exciting base games, *Golden Shield®* and *Jaguar King™*. Each of these games allows you to win free game bonuses, as well as two standalone progressive jackpots and a monetary bonus prize. The major jackpot starts at $200 and minor jackpot starts at $20.

59 - The *Jackpot Royale®* machine from Aristocrat

This game reminds me of the movie "300," which is based loosely on the motion picture "300 Spartans" that I saw many years ago as a young man. It's the story of the brave Spartans who held the mighty Persian army at bay at the Battle of Thermopylae in 480 BC. In one scene from that old movie the Spartan King Leonidas tricks the invading Persian cavalry by having his soldiers wait for the approaching horsemen, then lie on the ground covered by their golden shields. The invading cavalry does not have time to stop, and the horses simply jump over the Spartans. Once the cavalry passes over them, the Spartans get up and now have the invading Persian cavalry sandwiched between themselves at the back, and their brothers who were waiting in the wings. In this way they annihilate the Persian cavalry and chariots, and delay the advancement of the Persians. This delay gave the Athenians time to organize the Athenian and Spartan fleets, which then sailed to meet the Persian fleet and destroy it. It is the story of the golden shields that brought all of this to mind.

This slot machine game from Aristocrat is aptly named *Golden Shield*®, with the image of the Greek soldier prominently displayed on the machine's top box. In this game, you first select the number of lines you want to play and the bet value per each line you have chosen. All wins begin with leftmost reel and pay left to right on adjacent reels, except scatters. Each ACE and each GOLD ACE may change to GOLD ACE or ACE respectively once the reels spin.

Free Games Bonus Feature

You can win 20 Free games with any 3, 4 or 5 SHIELD symbols. This bonus feature can be triggered again during the bonus rounds. Credits bet and lines played are the same as the game that triggered the feature.

As in the game *Golden Shield*®, in *Jaguar King*® you first select the number of paylines you want to play, and the value of the bet per each payline selected. All wins begin with leftmost reel and pay left to right on adjacent reels, except scatters. Each ACE and each GOLD ACE may change to GOLD ACE or ACE respectively once the reels spin.

Free Games Bonus Feature

You can win 20 Free games with any 3, 4 or 5 STATUE symbols. This bonus feature can be triggered again during the bonus rounds. Credits bet and lines played are the same as the game that triggered the feature.

Jackpot Royale® Wins

You can win the Jackpot Royale® progressive prizes on both Golden Shield and Jaguar King. This occurs when the following combinations are hit:

- 5 of the GOLD ACE symbols win the Major Jackpot
- 4 of the GOLD ACE symbols win the Minor Jackpot
- 3 of the GOLD ACE symbols win a $20 Bonus Prize

Jackpot Royale® is different in that the higher your bet the more GOLD symbols appear. All of the *Jackpot Royale®* pays are left to right on adjacent and lit reels only. This means that you must activate all of the paylines in order to give yourself the best opportunity to hit these jackpots.

9

Bonus Games

Bonus games are the kind of machines that give you something "extra"—a "bonus"—for hitting specified symbols or combinations of symbols. There are many such games available, and all of them have a multitude of bonusing options. They are great fun to play, and the many bonuses offered mean that you will be getting wins at a very frequent rate. The range of such wins and special awards will keep you playing for a long time. There are also several jackpots and other such pays offered. All of this means not only more fun and longer play, but also bigger wins. Among the many great bonus games offered in the Aristocrat family are *Mr. Cashman®* and *Hit the Heights®*.

In 2002—and it all seems such a long time ago now—the world of slot machines was introduced to a brand-new friend called *Mr. Cashman®*. This friendly little fellow was soon to become extremely popular and to make many thousands of friends. The smiley little man with the top hat managed to give away so much money that everyone who knows him appreciates the frequent wins.

60 - The great and now venerable *Mr. Cashman®* slot machine from Aristocrat

Not only is *Mr. Cashman®* the player's best friend, he also appears randomly to give surprise bonus wins to lucky players. Dressed to the nines in top hat and gloves, *Mr. Cashman®* brings with him a wealth of credits and excitement with 5 different bonus features. Originally available on the games *Louie's Gold®* and *African Dusk®*, the game has also become available on many other titles, most recently in a new version called *Cashman Tonight®*, in the *VIRIDIAN*™ cabinet.

One of the best advantages of any *Mr. Cashman®* game is not only winning the random credits and all the bonuses, but also the fact that all of these pays and bonuses occur very frequently. You never know how soon you may win something, or how often you may win it! This game has a very high hit frequency, and the many wins that it offers can accumulate quite quickly.

Mr. Cashman® Bonus Features

The bonus feature consists of *Mr. Cashman®*, who will randomly appear and offer you the choice of five bonuses—provided you play with the ante bet. The total minimum bet to be eligible for the *Mr. Cashman®* feature is 30 credits. These extras awards are as follows:

Choose a Feature: Here you are prompted to touch the money bag, where you can win up to 1,000 credits, which are then multiplied by the bet per line on the game that started *Mr. Cashman®*; OR you can instead touch the gift box to win either 5, 10, 15 or 20 free games, during which all prizes will be multiplied by 2x, 3x or 5x the bet per line value.

61 - *Mr. Cashman®* Choose-A-Feature bonus screen

Random Spin: *Mr. Cashman®* randomly spins one or more reels, and then all wins are paid as per the pay table and also multiplied by 3x, 5x, or up to 10x the value.

62 - *Mr. Cashman®* Random Spin bonus screen

63 - *Mr. Cashman®* Random Bonus game screen

Random Bonus: Watch *Mr. Cashman®* give you a bonus prize. The highest available random prize is the top scorecard prize with a 10x multiplier. All of the other prizes are multiplied by the bet per line on the game that started *Mr. Cashman®*.

Match the Prize: Here you are prompted to touch the "star" symbols until 2 matching prizes have been revealed. You then win that prize. Your prize will be up to 1,000 credits, which are then multiplied by the bet per line on the game that started *Mr. Cashman®*; or you can instead choose 5, 10, 20, or 40 free games, during which wins will be multiplied by 1x, 2x, 3x or 5x the original wager amount respectively.

64 - *Mr. Cashman®* Match-the-Prize bonus screen

65 - *Mr. Cashman®* Poker Machine bonus screen

Poker Machine: You win the revealed bonus prize of up to 999 credits, which is then multiplied by the bet per line on the game that started *Mr. Cashman®*.

In addition, for every free game bonus or free spin bonus awarded by *Mr. Cashman®*, a prize of 2 credits—multiplied by the bet per line on the game that started

Mr. Cashman® and any other applicable multipliers—will be paid. There are a number of *Mr. Cashman*® games. *African Dusk*®, *Louie's Gold*®, and all other *Mr. Cashman*® titles are traditionally offered in the 1-cent and 2-cent denominations. In addition to the *Mr. Cashman*® features, each game offers a free game or scatter game bonus as well as the substitute symbols.

Hit the Heights® is a standalone bonus bet game that has been created to add a new level of excitement to gaming floors. This game has real drawing power with its eye-catching topper that interacts with the game during the Wheel Feature. The game has a very high hit frequency, meaning that you will hit the bonus features much more frequently than you might expect. There are 4 games in this family, including *Jungle Beat*™, *Space King*™, *Wild Ned*™ and *Wish Big!*™. These are either 25-line or 25-credit *Reel Power*® games with a 10-credit ante bet. Both versions require a minimum bet of 35-credits, and are offered predominately in low demoninations, with 175, 350 and 700 credit available max bet. You can see this distinctive game in Photo 66.

66 - The great *Hit the Heights*® bonus game from Aristocrat

The Sky's the Limit!

Many years ago—and it doesn't seem that long ago to me—there was a casino on the Las Vegas Strip called Vegas World. It was built, owned, and operated by Bob Stupak, a legendary Las Vegas gambler, entrepreneur, and visionary. I knew Bob, and spent time with him at Vegas World, in a little booth in the coffee shop that served as his de-facto office. I also spent time with him at his house, a sprawling old Las Vegas mansion with the décor to match. I wrote an article about him and his vision for "the tallest tower in the West." That was about 18 years ago. Bob died on September 25, 2009. He was one of the icons of Las Vegas, and I miss him and all of the old time Las Vegas pioneers like him.

I mention his story because at the front of Vegas World, Bob had a huge rocket pointed skyward with the slogan: The Sky's The Limit! That was his motto, and his knack for promotion. He once said that he would pay $1 million to anyone who would jump from the top of his casino and land safely. One such skydiver took him up on it, climbed to the top of the casino, jumped off, and landed safely in Bob's parking lot. Cameras rolling, Bob proudly presented the man with a check for $1 million—and then handed him a bill for $999,999.00—as the landing fee! So, for essentially $1, Bob got all of this publicity for his casino. That was Bob all right, and that's how he told me the story when I sat at his house one day.

Today, the Vegas World casino is history and the Stratosphere now stands in its place. Bob got his tower, and the world can thank Bob Stupak, and others like him, for making Las Vegas the greatest gambling city in the world. He was one of the best.

Speaking of the best, I first saw *Hit the Heights*® at the November 2009 gaming convention in Las Vegas, but by the time you read this book it will already be available in your favorite casino. Like Stupak's rocket, this game also reaches for the sky, and that's why it reminded me of Bob, his casino, his rocket, and his motto: The Sky's The Limit!

67 - The main game screen for *Hit the Heights*®, this one is from the *Wish Big!*™ game.

On all the four *Hit the Heights®* games you can enter the *Hit the Heights®* Wheel bonus, where you are prompted to touch the screen and launch rockets up to the video wheel in the top box.

68 - The *Hit the Heights®* Wheel Bonus main game bonus screens

69 - The *Hit the Heights®* Wheel Bonus wheel feature screen

This then shoots the rockets to the top screen, where the Hit the Heights Wheel Bonus is displayed on the second screen. That's why you will also see the screen with the prompt: "Look Up!" When the wheel is filled with possible prizes, it spins, shooting fireworks.

As the fireworks explode the dynamic prizes get bigger, and the higher you go up on the bonus levels displayed in lit symbols on the large top-box rocket. You'll understand this better once you see it, and it is truly a great sight! The length of firework explosions is random, increasing the anticipation of the win. If the fireworks stop on a credit prize, you win that prize. And if the fireworks stop on a *Hit the Heights®* prize you are awarded the *Hit the Heights®* Fireworks Bonus prize.

Apart from the Wheel bonuses, *Hit the Heights®* comes in 4 distinct game packages, each with its own special features, and bonuses. Here are the four games, a brief description of how each game works, and what is different about each one:

Wish Big™ is a 25-line game, with 35-credit minimum (25 per line + 10-credit ante bet). The game gives you the chance to win 10,15 or 20 Free Games with 3, 4 or 5 scattered GEM symbols. During the feature the *Wish Big*™ Wheel Bonus occurs after any win.

Wish Big!™ Wheel Feature

70 - The bonus screen on The *Wish Big!*™ game for *Hit the Heights*®

During the feature two wheels are displayed on the top screen. After any win you are prompted to select either the outer or inner wheel to spin the win multiplier. If a *WISH BIG!*™ segment is landed, the dice in the center of the wheel are rolled. The number rolled on the dice is the number of segments that are replaced with 25x (outer wheel) and 10x (inner wheel) segments. The wheel resets to one 25x (outer wheel) and 10x (inner wheel) segment for each free game. The feature can be triggered again while in the feature rounds.

Space King™ is a 25-credit *Reel Power*® game (25 reel credits plus 10-credit ante bet), and is also part of the *Hit the Heights*® family of games. The game gives you the chance to win the *Space King*™ Wheel Feature.

71 - The bonus screen on the *Space King*™ game for *Hit the Heights*®

Space King™ Wheel Feature

Any 4-of-a-kind picture symbols start the feature. The 4-of-a-kind trigger symbols are held and the remaining reel re-spun the number of times indicated on the wheel. A consolation prize of 20 credits is paid for non-winning trigger symbols during re-spin. WILD symbols substitute for all symbols during any re-spins. Dice appearing on the wheel indicate the number of additional spins of the wheel that will be awarded.

72 - The Wheel Bonus screen on *Space King*™ game for *Hit the Heights*®

Wild Ned™ is a 25-credit *Reel Power*® game (25 reel credits plus 10-credit ante bet), and is also part of the *Hit the Heights*® family of games. The game gives you the chance to win the *Wild Ned*™ Wheel Feature.

73 - The bonus screen on the *Wild Ned*™ game for *Hit the Heights*®

Wild Ned™ Wheel Feature

When you hit 3 or more scattered MINES, the free game feature is started. You can choose to play 5, 8 or 12 free games. The fewer free games you choose, the more dice you will get on the wheel. During the free games "Wild Ned" wins are multiplied by the wheel value. When the "Roll Dice" segment is spun, the dice are rolled in the center of the wheel and all wheel numbers are multiplied by this value for the current "Wild Ned" win.

74 - The Wheel Feature bonus screen on the *Wild Ned*™ game for *Hit the Heights*®

For some reason I always want to call this game Jungle *Beast*—although it is really called *Jungle Beat*™. I guess—as Elvis Presley once said in a movie—"It's just the beast in me." I once hit the top level on the rocket topper in this game, but I must admit it was during the convention so I didn't get to take the win home with me. But it was great to see it, anyway. That's exactly the kind of win you can get when playing this game in your favorite casino. This is a 25-line game, with 35-credit minimum (25 per line + 10 credit ante bet).

75 - The bonus screen on the *Jungle Beat*™ game for *Hit the Heights*®

Jungle Beat™ Wheel Feature

76 - The Wheel Bonus game on *Jungle Beat*™ for *Hit the Heights*®

The Bonus Feature is triggered with 3 or more scattered DRUM symbols. Every time a WHEEL symbol is spun up on reel 3, the wheel in the top monitor spins and then any applicable wins are paid. The WHEEL in the top monitor will award WILD symbols which remain WILD for the duration of the feature, extra free games, or a credit prize. The feature cannot be triggered again while in the feature itself.

And this, my friends, is the story of the *Hit the Heights*® game, and the story of my old friend Bob, Vegas World, the rocket, and the tower ....

10

Progressive Games DSAP & TSAP

Progressive games can be found in linked products as well as in standalone games. The letters DSAP stand for Double Standalone Progressive; the letters TSAP stand for Triple Standalone Progressive; and the letters SAP stand for Standalone Progressive. These are all different versions of progressive games. "Stand alone" simply means that all the progressives are contained within that one machine, and are not linked to any other machine or games, either within that casino or among many casinos. This differentiates these games from the others I have mentioned in this book. "Standalone progressive" means that the game has one jackpot which is usually located on the screen. In a Double Standalone Progressive, the game has two jackpots, both of which are progressives and usually located in the top box. Most of the time, one of the jackpots is considered as Major and the second as Minor. When the machine is a Triple Standalone Progressive, there are three jackpots available on that one machine and located in the top box. Usually they are called Major, Minor, and the Mini.

These are all progressives, meaning that they have a specific seed value amount at which the jackpots begin to grow—known as the start-up value (or "seed" amount)—and they continue to grow incrementally as the machine is being played, until they are hit. When they are hit, they automatically reset to the start value, plus any hidden increments, and the process is repeated as the jackpot continues to grow from that point. Among the most popular games in these categories is a derivative of the *Mr. Cashman*® games, called: *Cashman Tonight*®.

Aristocrat Technologies is proud to present *Cashman Tonight*®, a Double Standalone Progressive which is an exciting extension of the *Mr. Cashman*® brand of gaming machines. Combining the allure of two standalone progressive jackpots with the popular *Mr. Cashman*® bonus features, *Cashman Tonight*® adds a new dimension to the games players love. Any one of five bonus features may appear randomly during play when you play the max lines plus the *Cashman*™ Bonus bet. This game is one of those that are called "bonus bet" games, meaning you have to wager the additional amount in order to be eligible for the extra pays and bonuses. The features include Scatter Games, Match a Prize, *Wild Lights*™, *Love Meter*™, and *Cash Wheel*™. Everything from free games to interactive "pick your prize" options are present in these bonus rounds.

77 - The *Cashman Tonight*® Double Standalone Progressive game from Aristocrat

A number of titles, including *African Dusk*®, *Claim the Throne*™ and *Arctic Wins*®, are available in the *Cashman Tonight*® lineup. The games are configured as 20 lines plus a 10-cent ante bet with a max bet of 300 credits.

In *African Dusk*™, the RHINO symbol substitutes for all other symbols, and the scattered TREE symbols pay in any position. All wins are shown in credits, except major and minor jackpot meter amounts.

In the *Claim the Throne*™ game, the PRINCE symbol substitutes for all other symbols, except scatters. Every PRINCE symbol that substitutes in a win doubles the pay for that win, and the PRINCE symbols appear on reels 2, 3 and 4 only.

Cashman Tonight® Bonus

In addition to all the bonuses offered on each of the games available in the *Cashman Tonight*® family of games, you can also qualify for the *Cashman Tonight*® Bonus. In order to do this, you must play maximum lines + the CASHMAN BONUS. *Mr. Cashman*® will randomly appear at the end of a bought game to give you one of 5 available bonus features, which are as follows:

Scatter Game

You will win 1 free game where *all symbols* will pay scattered in any position. Prizes for all symbols—except the regular SCAT-

TER symbols—are multiplied by the bet per line on the game that started this *Cashman Tonight®* Bonus. The SCAT-TER wins are multiplied by the number of lines played times the bet per line. Each winning combination is made up of only one symbol from each reel.

78 - The *Cashman Tonight®* Scatter Game bonus screen

Match A Prize

In this game you will see a screen full of suitcase symbols, and you will be asked to choose a CASE symbol until 2 matching prizes have been revealed. Prizes available are from 50 to 400 credits (times the bet per line on the game that started the *Cashman Tonight®* Bonus as shown on the screen). You win the matched prize multiplied by any revealed multipliers, which can be either 2x, 3x, 4x, or 5x the amount.

79 - The *Cashman Tonight®* Match-a-Prize Game bonus screens

Wild Lights™

In this game you will win 3 free games, and during each free game the *WILD LIGHTS*™ symbols may be placed on one random position. The *WILD LIGHTS*™ symbols remain in the same position until free games have been completed. During these free games all such *WILD LIGHTS*™ symbols substitute for all other symbols.

80 - The *Cashman Tonight®* *Wild Lights*™ bonus screen

Love Meter™

In this game you will see a screen where *Mr. Cashman*® gives you your choice of four cute *Cashgirl*™ symbols. You are then prompted to touch your selected *Cash-girl*™ symbol. You then win that prize, and the amount of that prize is then displayed on the *Love Meter*™. It can be anything from 20 to 400 credits times the bet per line on the game that started the *Cashman Tonight*® bonus. This prize will also be multiplied by the final value

81 - The *Cashman Tonight*® *Love Meter*™ bonus screen

of the Love Arrow. You have the option to forfeit the first prize won and instead pick another *Cashgirl*™. To do this you can either touch the "TAKE WIN" or "PLAY AGAIN" options.

Cash Wheel™

In this game you will be asked to touch 6 boxes to fill in the blank spaces on the wheel. Prizes available behind the boxes are credit prizes or free games with multipliers. Touch PLAY or press "*Cashman Tonight*® Bonus Repeat Bet" button to start the *Cash Wheel*™. You will win whatever prize is displayed when the *Cash Wheel*™ stops. If the wheel stops on the MAJOR or MINOR jackpots, you will then win that corresponding jackpot.

82 - The *Cashman Tonight*® *Cash Wheel*™ bonus screens

For every free game awarded by the *Cashman Tonight*® Bonus, a prize of 2 credits multiplied by the bet per line on the game that started the *Cashman Tonight*® bonus, and any other applicable multipliers, will be given if no other win occurs, and the bet per line and number of lines played will be the same as that for the game that started the *Cashman Tonight*® bonus.

This Double Standalone Progressive game is a fantastic addition to the *Sun & Moon*® series. It features all the elements of the original successful video game, coupled with the addition of two standalone jackpots, which can be won when playing maximum bet. All wins begin with leftmost reel and pay left to right on adjacent reels, including scatters. The SUN symbol substitutes for all symbols, except the MOON; the MOON symbol substitutes for all symbols except the SUN. One of the major differences of this game is that you have to play max bet to win the jackpot, and both jackpots are static at $100 on a 1c game.

83 - The *Sun&
Moon*® *Total
Eclipse* machine
from Aristocrat

84 - Play max bet for your chance to win the jackpots

Free Games Bonus Feature

You can win 5, 10, 20 or 50 free games when 2, 3, 4 or 5 scattered SUN, MOON, (or mixed) symbols occur respectively, from leftmost reel to right.

Sun & Moon® Total Eclipse Feature

During the free games, all *Sun & Moon®* symbols on reels 1, 2, 3 and 4 only become ECLIPSE symbols. The ECLIPSE symbols substitute for all other symbols. When playing the MAX BET option, the scattered ECLIPSE - ECLIPSE - ECLIPSE - ECLIPSE - SUN symbol combination wins the SUN PROGRESSIVE top jackpot.

85 - The Sun Progressive bonus screen

The scattered ECLIPSE - ECLIPSE - ECLIPSE - ECLIPSE - MOON symbol combination wins the MOON PROGRESSIVE top jackpot.

86 - The Moon Progressive
bonus screen

Although I would advise you to do so, you don't have to play the game at max bet. This is your choice. If you are *not* playing the game with max bet, you will instead have the chance to win as follows:

- Scattered ECLIPSE - ECLIPSE - ECLIPSE - ECLIPSE - SUN symbol combination now wins 25x your total bet; and
- The Scattered ECLIPSE - ECLIPSE - ECLIPSE - ECLIPSE - MOON combination now wins 25x your total bet.

As you can see, you can still win a very good amount even if you do not play at max bet. Nevertheless, by means of strategy advice, I would be remiss if I did not remind you, one more time, that playing any game without the wagers and bets necessary to actually win the jackpot is highly inadvisable. Even though it is possible, and on these great games you can still get good wins, you are not giving yourself an opportunity to have the game perform for you to its optimum potential if you don't play it with the jackpot-bet requirements.

Outback Jack®

It's more than a game... It's an adventure! There are 6 exciting second screen bonus features as well as the progressive jackpots. *Outback Jack*® is one of the great performers in the *Double Standalone Progressive* family. The six possible bonus features are comprised of such Aussie expeditions as Nippy Surf, Winding River, Great Sandy Desert, Gold Mine, and the *Outback Jack*® Card Feature. In these bonus rounds, you may be awarded free games, credits, multipliers, or one of the two progressive jackpots. *Outback Jack*® is a 20-line game, with a 10-credit ante bet. Max

87 - The *Outback Jack*® *Double Standalone Progressive* game from Aristocrat

bet options are 300 or 600 credits. The game is available in predominantly low denominations, with payback return percentages between 91 and 93 percent. So, as Australians would say: "She's a beauty, mate!"

Outback Jack® Bonus

You must play maximum lines plus the *Outback Jack®* Bonus bet in order to be eligible for the *Outback Jack®* Bonus. The *Outback Jack®* Bonus is triggered when the bonus bet is made and three or more MAP symbols appear on the screen. Which of the 6 *Outback Jack®* Bonus features you get is selected at random.

Winding River Bonus Game

Try to get *Outback Jack®* across the river. You are asked to touch a rock with a YELLOW prize. If *Outback Jack®* stays on the rock, the prize is added to the Current Prize Pool, and you can then make another selection. If *Outback Jack®* falls into the water, the game is over and the Current Prize Pool credits are awarded. If you make it to the other side, the Current Prize Pool credits are DOUBLED, and then awarded. A consolation prize of 75 credits—times the number of credits bet per line in the game that started the *Outback Jack®* Bonus—is awarded if *Outback Jack®* falls off the first rock. Prizes

88 - *Outback Jack®* Winding River Bonus game screen

shown are for a 1-credit bet per line multiplied by the credits bet per line in the game that started the *Outback Jack®* Bonus.

Nippy Surf Bonus Game

Touch a Board that you want *Outback Jack®* to ride. As *Outback Jack®* rides the wave, the prize increases as shown on the

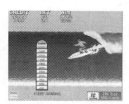

89 - *Outback Jack*®
Nippy Surf Bonus
game screen

screen. If *Outback Jack*® falls into the water, the game is over and the indicated prize is awarded. If *Outback Jack*® rides the wave into the shore, a bonus prize is added to the indicated prize and both prizes are awarded. Prizes shown are for a 1-credit bet per line multiplied by the credits bet per line in the game that started the *Outback Jack*® Bonus.

Big Rock Bonus Game

The "big rock" referred to in this bonus is the famous Australian landmark once called Ayers Rock, which is now known more by its Aboriginal name: Uluru. The "rock" is located in Australia's Northern Territory, in Uluru-Kata Tjuta National Park, about 350 km (around 218 miles) southwest of Alice Springs. If you're ever in Australia, pay a visit to this famous

90 - *Outback Jack*®
Big Rock Bonus game
screen

landmark, as it is well worth it. You will also get to throw a boomerang, which is what *Outback Jack*® is doing in this bonus, where you can win up to 2,000 credits, multiplied by credits bet per line on the game that started the *Outback Jack*® Bonus.

Gold Mine Bonus Game

In this bonus, *Outback Jack*® automatically digs twice for prizes as indicated on the prizes-found meter. You can then continue to touch the screen for the dig either to continue or stop, at which point you can leave to exit the bonus. If you choose to leave, the prizes you have found so far are won. If you continue to dig and the cave does not collapse, the new prizes are added to the prizes

already found. But if you continue to dig
and the cave collapses, only half the prizes found are awarded (rounded up to the
nearest credit), and the feature ends. This
is the "risk vs. reward" bonus option. Prizes
shown are for a 1-credit bet per line, multiplied by the credits bet per line in the game
that started the *Outback Jack®* Bonus. You
can take a chance by touching the DIG option up to a maximum of 6 times.

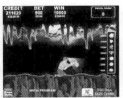

91 - *Outback Jack®*
Gold Mine Bonus
game screen

Fishing Spot Bonus Game

92 - *Outback Jack®*
Fishing Spot Bonus
game screen

In this bonus, you can win up to 7
free games. Prizes are awarded for 5 scatters. An additional 7 Free Games can be
won when 5 scattered PRAWNS symbols
hit during the feature. The MARLIN substitutes for the BARRAMUNDI, TUNA,
BARRACUDA, MAHI and TARPON
symbols.

Great Sandy Desert Bonus Game

93 - *Outback Jack®* Great
Sandy Desert bonus
game screen

In this bonus you can win up to 15
Free Games. The BOOMERANG symbol
substitutes for all other symbols, except the
KANGAROO symbols. Scattered KAN-
GAROO symbols pay in any position, and
any winning combination containing one
or more BOOMERANG symbols is multiplied by 2x, 3x, 5x or 10x as indicated on
the screen. This bonus cannot be triggered
again during the bonus rounds. The bet per
line and the number of lines played are the same as the game that
started the *Outback Jack®* bonus.

Outback Jack® Card Feature

The *Outback Jack*® card feature can be won at random during any bought game. Once the feature is won, touch the CARD symbols of your choice. Match the cards (as shown on the screen) to win the corresponding progressive jackpot, or the 500-credit prize. These wins are as follows:

- ANY 5 or more *Outback Jack*® symbols win the MAJOR Progressive Jackpot (Level l);
- ANY 4 SHARKS symbols win the MINOR Progressive Jackpot (Level 2);
- ANY 3 CROCODILES symbols win the 500 Credit Prize

94 - *Outback Jack*® Card Bonus game screen

If a ROO Card is revealed, any CROC Cards displayed on screen at the time become *Outback Jack*® Cards. A maximum of two ROO Cards can appear in any card feature.

I have spent a lot of time in Australia, and enjoyed every bit of it. I can tell you from personal experience that the symbols, and bonus rounds, in this game accurately represent much of the fun for which Australians are famous. While in America we tend to identify Australians with the now famous slogan "Put a shrimp on the barbie," this tends to irritate Australians no end because in Australia a "shrimp" is called a "prawn." So instead of saying "Put a shrimp on the barbie," you should probably get into the habit of saying "Pick a prawn, mate!" At least this way you will sound a lot more Australian, which may help you when playing *Outback Jack*® and enjoying all the bonuses and pays that this game has to offer.

Banana King®

Banana King® is an exciting new *Double Standalone Progressive*, meaning you can win one of two progressive jackpots on the game. When playing max lines plus the *Banana King®* bet, you become eligible to win one of five bonus features: *Wild King™*, *Great Race™*, *Banana Match™*, *Cash Climb™*, and *Coco Bingo™*. In these bonus rounds, you may win free games, bonus credits, and multipliers. The Match Card Progressive Jackpot feature can be won randomly during any paid game, and provides a chance to play the card feature to win one of the two progressive jackpots, or a consolation prize.

And the best news? You can win on this machine without having to compete with other players, because this progressive is just for each machine, and not linked to others. So, you can always look for the good progressive amounts, and not only enjoy the great base game, and

95 - The *Panther Magic™ Banana King®* slot machine from Aristocrat

the many bonuses, but also the healthy jackpots. There are several themes in the *Banana King®* family of games, including *Dolphin Treasure®*, *Wild Ways®*, *Panther Magic™, Turtle Treasure®* and *Shaman's Magic®*.

The games are configured as 25 lines or 25 credits for *Reel Power®* games plus a 10-cent ante bet. The Minor jackpot starts at $50, and the Major jackpot starts at $750.

Go Ape, Young Man!

With apologies to Horace Greeley for paraphrasing his famous "Go West, young man!" slogan, let us understand that this wonderful game from Aristocrat is for all the ladies as well as all the men. Young—or as old as me (ehm, let's not get into *that* just this moment!)—the point is well taken: This is a 25-line double stand-alone progressive, with *two* progressive jackpots, not just one. The 5 bonuses that you can win on all *Banana King®* games—when you play with the ante bet—are as follows:

Wild King™

In this feature, three free games are won. During each free game a *Banana King®* will be placed randomly on the screen over an entire reel position and substitutes for all symbols. Each *Banana King®* remains in the same reel position for the remaining free games.

96 - The *Banana King® Wild King*™ Bonus game screens

97 - The *Banana King®* Great Race Bonus game screen

Great Race

Here you get to pick a character for the Animal Race. What you win then depends on where your character placed in the race: the better the result, the more you win. So, cheer for your pick, and urge your animal on!

Banana Match

Here you have a screen full of bananas. You get to pick as many BANANAS as you can until two prizes match. Wins may be multiplied by 2, 5 or 10 times.

98 - The *Banana King*® Banana Match Bonus game screen

Climb 4 Cash

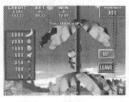

99 - The *Banana King*® Climb 4 Cash Bonus game screen

You didn't think this was going to be easy, did you? Here you have to climb up the tree to win prizes. But you don't have to climb the tree yourself—the monkey will do it for you. As the monkey climbs the tree, you can choose to keep climbing—or leave with whatever you have already won. If you choose to keep climbing and the monkey falls off the tree, you will collect only half of the prizes you have won up to that point. So, don't fall off—right?

Coco Bingo

100 - The *Banana King*® Coco Bingo Bonus game screen

In this feature you get to press the PLAY button and random BINGO COCONUTS will automatically be selected. When an entire row of 5 coconuts in a straight line (vertically, horizontally or diagonally) has been selected, the total of the prizes and multipliers revealed in that row will be paid to you and multiplied by credits per line played. You can win up to 220 credits (multiplied by the number on the bet button as shown on the screen), and these wins may be multiplied by 2, 3 or 4.

Match Card Jackpot Feature

101 - The *Banana King*®
Match Card Bonus game
screen

The Match Card jackpot feature can be won at random after any spin and is your way to winning the jackpots. The screen fills up with cards to choose from. Match cards to win the corresponding Progressive Jackpot, or the 1,000 credit prize.

So, there you have it. *Banana King*®. Yes, indeed, Go Ape!

11

Licensed Games

As you may remember, in Chapter One I discussed the meaning of the various terms in the gaming industry. The term "licensed games" refers to those games that are created and owned by third parties. This simply means that the manufacturer of the slot machine has entered into a licensing agreement with the designers and/or owners of that particular concept, and under that license they have developed a slot game based on that theme. For example, the first game I will introduce in this chapter is based on the popular television series *The Sopranos*®. This *HBO*® television series is owned by the show's creators and the network, under their own contractual agreements. When Aristocrat wanted to create a slot machine based on this show and its theme, they entered into a licensing agreement with the owners of *The Sopranos*®. Under that agreement Aristocrat was then able to create a slot machine that includes the characters, themes, and other stories and imagery ideas that are embodied in the show, and *The Sopranos'*® creative concept.

This arrangement applies to all machines and games shown in this chapter, as well as to any game that is based on a theme that has perhaps become iconic pop-culture, or is something with which we are all familiar but was not specifically created by the designers directly for the slot machine manufacturer. Of course, this does not affect the game, or the game's performance. It simply explains how the game came to be and why it is called a "licensed" product in the industry. This is a way to bring more gaming entertainment to the casino, and to give you—the player—more choices to play games whose themes may already be familiar to you.

Let's begin with *The Sopranos*®, a game that comes in many versions. I will highlight two: *Respect the Bing*™ and *This Thing of Ours*™.

The Sopranos®

So good it's criminal! Settle in for some great wins, 'cause the Boss said so! You got it? Good! Well, that's about as much of this kind of movie-speak as I can stand. It's fun to make fun, especially if you remember a movie called "Nicky Blue Eyes." But this is a slot machine, based on the very popular TV show: *The Sopranos*®. It is gaming's new top boss, a Double Standalone Progressive video slot machine that is part of a big family of Aristocrat slots. *The Sopranos*® has a double-standalone progressive and offers five exciting bonus features, where you get "made" with free credits, games, multipliers and progressive jackpots. The base is a 20-line plus 10-credit ante bet format.

If you ever wanted to take a trip "on the wild side" and step into the world of "The Godfather" or "Casino," both great movies of the same genre as *The Sopranos*®, then this is the game for you.

There are two kinds of games available under the general Sopranos theme. One is called *Respect the Bing*™ and the other is called *This Thing of Ours*™. The really cool things about these games are the great video clips that play throughout the game. They are actual clips from the show itself, so if you're a fan of the TV show, you'll get an extra kick out of these clips! And if you're not a fan of the show, or aren't familiar with the TV version of *The Sopranos*®, you will be introduced to a cast of characters that are truly from "Back East." And if you aren't in tune with contemporary American pop-culture, don't fret either, because these video clips will make it clear what the game is all about.

102 - *The Sopranos*®
Respect the Bing™
slot machine from
Aristocrat

103 - *The Sopranos*®
This Thing of Ours™
slot machine from
Aristocrat

Both games offer Double Standalone Progressive jackpots, meaning that each of *The Sopranos*® games has two jackpots. The Capo jackpot starts at $25, and the Boss jackpot starts at $250.

104 - Examples of *The Sopranos*® video clips

When you make the bonus bet, you will trigger the random selection of any one of the following five bonuses:

- Roulette Wheel
- Scatter Game
- Truck Heist
- Pick Your Earner
- Dancer Bonus

105 - *The Sopranos*® Roulette Wheel bonus screen

106 - *The Sopranos*® Scatter Game bonus screen

107 - *The Sopranos*® Truck Heist bonus screen

108 - *The Sopranos*® Pick
Your Earner bonus screen

109 - *The Sopranos*® Dancer
Bonus screen

In the Roulette Wheel bonus, you can win one of the progressive jackpots, free games or credit prizes. In the Scatter Game,
you get one free game where *all* symbols pay anywhere in the window. In the Truck Heist feature there is a bonus that allows you to
match two trucks to win a prize, and a possible multiplier. The Pick
Your Earner Bonus is where you can choose an earner to win free
credits and multiplier, and in the Dancer Bonus you win three free
games, where during each free game a *Wild Lights*™ symbol may be
added to one position on the reels.

As you can see, this is truly a great game. So let's go—I'll "take
you for a ride." Good luck!

Jeff Foxworthy™ *Redneck Rumble*™

I have always been a great fan of Jeff Foxworthy. He is an extremely funny man, and I just loved all of those TV specials where
he would tell those "you might be a redneck if—" humorous anec-
dotes. I remember a few of them:

- "If you've ever taken a beer to a job interview, you might be a redneck."
- "If improving your house means putting on new tires, you might be a redneck."
- "If you consider a six pack of beer and a bug zapper as quality entertainment, you might be a redneck."

Those are just a few of the pearls of wisdom I happen to remember from the comedy specials that Jeff Foxworthy has produced and starred in. It is precisely this kind of great all-American humor that has made Jeff so successful, and so loved by people everywhere. It was, therefore, inevitable that his success would find its way into one of the most humorous slot machines ever made—now available in your favorite casino.

110 - The *Jeff Foxworthy*™ *Redneck Rumble*™ slot machine from Aristocrat

Here's how the game works: It is a *Triple Standalone Progressive* video slot game, where all wins pay left to right only on adjacent reels, except scatters. You must play maximum lines and the FOX-WORTHY BONUS bet in order to be eligible for all of the features and bonuses. The bet for the FOXWORTHY BONUS is 30 lines + 10 credits bonus bet, multiplied by the bet per line. During the base game the TROPHY Symbol substitutes for all symbols except for the TV!

111 - The *Jeff Foxworthy*™ *Redneck Rumble*™ main game screen, with the three progressives

The game has 3 jovial bonus features: Truck-O-War, Stink Bait Bonus or Foxworthy Free-For-All, plus the progressive Backyard Beer Hunt jackpot feature. This very entertaining game will surely bring a smile as you play it, just as Jeff Foxworthy's humor has brought a smile to millions of people all over the world.

Bonus Features

The Foxworthy Bonus is triggered when three or more TV scatters appear on the screen. This occurs on average 1 in every 40 spins. The Foxworthy Bonus feature is selected at random from Truck-O-War, Stink Bait Bonus, or Foxworthy Free-For-All.

112 - The *Jeff Foxworthy*™ Bonus game screen

Truck-O-War Bonus Feature

Just like tug of war but with trucks! You have 3 chances to choose which driver will win a Truck-O-War. After choosing a driver, while the Truck-O-War continues, the prize-o-meter increases. If your chosen driver wins, you are awarded the amount indicated on the prize-o-meter. If your chosen driver loses, the prize-o-meter returns to the previous value. When 3 contests have been completed, or the prize-o-meter reaches its maximum value, the Truck-O-War feature ends and the credit values, pointed to by the prize-o-meter, are awarded.

113 - The *Jeff Foxworthy*™ Truck-O-War Bonus game screen

Stink Bait Bonus Feature

In this bonus you get to cast a fishing line into a redneck's backyard pool, trying to catch fish with associated prize values.

114- The *Jeff Foxworthy*™ Stink Bait Bonus game screen

After the second cast, you have the option to cast again, or take your winnings. Each additional item caught adds to the winnings, but if you cast again and catch the plug hole, you are awarded only half of the prizes accumulated to that point and the feature ends. This is the same principle of risk vs. reward that I described earlier for the game *Chicken2*™. In the Stink Bait Bonus feature for the *Jeff Foxworthy*™ game you can cast up to 8 times, and if you get it right all 8 casts, you may receive a really nice win!

Foxworthy Free-For-All Bonus Feature

Here you can win up to 10 free games. Any winning combination containing one or more TROPHY symbols is multiplied by 2, 3, 5 or 10, as indicated. Any 3 or more TV symbols award 10 more free games. Lines played and bet multiplier are the same as the game that started the Foxworthy Bonus. The TROPHY symbol substitutes for all symbols, except TV.

Jackpot Feature - Backyard Beer Hunt

The Progressive jackpots can be won any time at random, offering you entry into the Backyard Beer Hunt. Once you enter the feature you are asked to touch 5 objects from the backyard, where you win 1 to 5 CANS, a credit prize, or 5 MORE PICKS. The number of cans collected determines which of the progressives you will win, or if you will win the consolation prize of 400 credits.

If CANS symbols are revealed, the CAN counter is incremented by the number of CANS. If a credit prize is revealed, you win that prize. If 5 MORE PICKS is revealed you are awarded 5 extra choices. At the end of the feature, prizes are awarded as follows, and as indicated by the CAN counter:

- 29 or more CANS wins the MAJOR jackpot.
- 21 to 28 CANS wins the MINOR jackpot.
- 10 to 20 CANS wins the MINI jackpot.
- 9 or fewer CANS wins 400 credits.

115 - The *Jeff Foxworthy*™ jackpot Bonus—Backyard Beer Hunt game screen

And so, you might be a redneck, too! Beer, anyone?

JAWS™

Based on the exciting book by Peter Benchley and the 1976 Academy Award®™ winning film franchise, the *JAWS*™ slot machine is a total interactive experience. Go Ahead—Take a Bite! No, this shark doesn't bite ... it gives 3 separate Bonuses, plus a *Hyperlink*® Jackpot feature as well as a base game feature that gives you that feeling of getting something—like money! If you are lucky. Yes, it's true that when you hit the bonus round, the machine you are playing turns blood red— but, unlike in the movie, here the big shark is about to give *you* some wins. It's an awesome game, now in casinos everywhere.

116 - The unmistakable *JAWS*™ slot machine from Aristocrat

JAWS™ is a 4-level, linked progressive jackpot product, and is available as a fully themed game package. The themed *VIRIDIAN*™ cabinet features a buoy topper, water trim, shark tooth bash button, shark gill speaker covers, edge lighting and resonates the unmistakable *JAWS*™ soundtrack—DaaaDa, DaaaDa. The high volatility base games are fully *JAWS*™ themed and 4 bonus features create a high bonus frequency for all players, delivering an unforgettable experience. The game is available in low denominations, with a 35-credit bet (25 +10-credit ante bet) base game.

Apart from the 3 bonus features and the *Hyperlink*® Jackpots, there is also a Base Game Bonus Feature, where you can choose 5, 10 or 20 free games, or the Dice Bonus. In the Dice Bonus, you can increase your multiplier by accumulating the most "Shark" dice rolled during the dice games. The main bonuses are as follows:

Golden JAWS™ Bonus Feature

In this bonus you are asked to touch the shark's teeth, and accumulate credits. After touching 3 teeth you can choose to continue to touch teeth and accumulate additional credits, or you can

take the credits already won. If you continue to touch teeth and the shark mouth closes, you win only half of the credits won so far. This is the "risk vs. reward" feature, meaning you have the choice of continuing with the bonus and trying for a bigger bonus win, but at the risk of half of the credits you have already won. So, if the shark's

117 - The Golden *JAWS*™ bonus screen

mouth does not close on you, you win more money. But if it does "bite" you, well, at least you still have half of the bonus—so not all is lost. Maybe a little pride, but you still have your fingers.

Shark Hunter Bonus

A bit like *Battleship*® the board game, here you are asked to choose 1, 2, 5, 10 or 15 chances to find the shark. The more chances you choose, the less the prize is for finding the shark. A "Fish Finder" screen with 20 positions is displayed. You then touch the screen to make your selections and keep touching until either the shark is found or you have used up all your picks. If you do not find the shark, a consolation prize is won.

118 - The *JAWS*™ Shark Hunter Bonus screen

Feeding Time Bonus

119 - The *JAWS*™ Feeding Time Bonus screen

In this bonus, 20 icons are displayed on the screen at the beginning of the feature. You must choose 2 icons to reveal your prize, but once the feature starts, the icons begin to disappear at random, no longer making those prizes available. Speed, therefore, is the trick of this bonus. Pick fast, or you'll get eaten!

Jackpot Bonus Feature

And then there is the Jackpot Bonus Feature. This jackpot feature is *randomly* triggered during *any* bought game. Once this

120 - The *JAWS*™ Jackpot Bonus screen

happens, you will receive 30 free spins. Each SHARK or BOAT symbol spun up during the free spins moves the SHARK or BOAT game piece around the game board respectively. A jackpot is won when the SHARK and BOAT meet on the same space, and the space achieved determines which level of jackpot is awarded. If the SHARK and BOAT do not meet after 30 spins, the Mini jackpot is still awarded, so once you get into this bonus Jackpot round, you are assured of winning at least the Mini.

And just as you thought it was safe to go back in the water, here comes the most recent addition to the *JAWS*™ link—*JAWS*™ the *Night Hunter*™! The shark is back, and this time, he's hunting at night. Like its predecessor, *JAWS*™, *Night Hunter*™ is based on the Academy Award® ™ winning film franchise, and completely submerges you in a total experience.

121 - The *JAWS*™ *Night Hunter*™ slot machine from Aristocrat

JAWS™ *Night Hunter*™ is a 50-line, one-credit-buys-2-lines game. *JAWS*™ *Night Hunter*™ is alive with stunning graphics and amazing sound, giving you an experience that's even more fun than a day at the beach. But the real action begins when three scattered *JAWS*™ trigger the base game feature. A second screen feature appears where you are given a choice of 4 options, as follows:

- 7 free games feature with *Sticky Wild*® symbols;
- 5 Dice Games with Prizes Multiplied by 2, 3 or 5;
- 3 Dice Games with prizes multiplied by 3, 5 or 8; or
- The most volatile option, the 1 Dice Game with prizes multiplied by 10, 15 or 25.

Just like the original *JAWS*™ game, *Night Hunter*™ brings back all those familiar bonus features, such as the Golden Jaw, Shark Hunter and Feeding Time bonuses. There's also the familiar Jackpot Bonus Feature, a "board game" that is randomly triggered during any bought game.

So, are you feeling adventurous? Feel like taking a dip? Maybe that vacation to the beach should instead include a visit to your favorite casino, where you can find either the original *JAWS*™ game, or the brand new *JAWS*™ *Night Hunter*™ game. Either way, go ahead—take a bite! After all, the jackpots are there, the bonuses are there, so what's keeping you? Oh, you mean that big ole shark? Just sit back and enjoy the bite—er, I mean ride. Just a little "biting" humor. Did I hear you say "very little humor"?

Kentucky Derby™

Kentucky Derby™ is an *RFX*™ stepper link progressive with 2 support games—*Run for the Roses*™ and *Oaks Day*™. The link has a 3-level single-site progressive and a static Grand Jackpot, meaning that all four jackpots are self-contained on the machines in the same bank.

Single site progressive means just that, as opposed to multi-site progressive where jackpots are won among players in different casinos, such as those within the state or even across state lines, depending on the regulations in the local jurisdictions.

With the various bonuses and choices available in these

122 - The *Kentucky Derby*™ single site progressive slot machine from Aristocrat

games, you have more of a chance of being one of the lucky winners of at least one of these 4 jackpots.

Kentucky Derby™ **Bonus**

You will win 15 free games when 3 or more HORSESHOE symbols occur on the screen. You are then prompted to choose 3 numbers corresponding to horses in the race. You are able to then watch the race in the top screen. During the feature you touch the BINOCULARS symbols to reveal a "Race Bonus credit," and one of your horses will move forward in the race. For each game where

the BINOCULARS do not appear, a competitor horse is randomly selected to move forward. On the last free game, one of your horses may be randomly selected to move forward one or more positions. The Major, Minor and Mini jackpots are won according to your result in the horse race.

123 - The *Kentucky Derby*™ Bonus screen

Major Jackpot

The major jackpot is won when your selected horses finish 1st, 2nd and 3rd in the order in which you selected them.

Minor Jackpot

The minor jackpot is won when your selected horses finish 1st , 2nd and 3rd, but not necessarily in the order in which you have selected them.

Mini Jackpot

The mini jackpot is won when your selected horses finish 1st and 2nd in any order selected.

Race Bonus

124 - The *Kentucky Derby*™ Race Bonus winners' screen

An additional prize is the Race Bonus, which is won at the end of the race. If you horse finishes 1ˢᵗ, the Race Bonus meter amount is multiplied by 2, 3, 5 or 10.

124 (a) - The *Kentucky Derby*™
Race Bonus game screen

Grand Jackpot

The Grand Jackpot remains static at $10,000, and this jackpot is awarded when you play at max bet level, and receive 5 binoculars on each reel. This jackpot can occur either in the base game, or within the bonus. So, off to the races, everyone!

12

Linked Progressive Games

When we speak about linked progressive games, we mean that all the games on the bank are linked together and contribute towards the jackpots. There are 2 types of linked progressives, Single Site Progressives (SSP) and Multi site Progressives (MSP). Multi Site Progressives are also known as Wide area Progressives (WAP), meaning that machines are linked between many different casinos (depending on the jurisdictions where this is permitted). Examples of Multi-Site Progressives are links such as *Millioni$er®* and *Mega Millioni$er®*. Single Site Progressive means that those games are linked together in a bank of machines in the *same* casino (an example is *Cash Express®*).

The way you can identify these links is that they are always in a group, known as a "bank of machines," and they all share common progressives which can be won by any player playing on any machine in that identified group. The more players that are playing them, the higher the jackpots grow. These jackpots can get very big; in the case of many of the Multi Site Progressives they can grow to over $1 million. There are, of course, many other jackpots available, such as the Mini, Minor and Major, or other similarly identified progressives available on these machines.

A progressive usually has a meter, and on this meter the amount of the jackpot continues to grow as the games are being played, until such time as someone hits the combination that awards them one—or possibly more than one—of these progressive jackpots. How these jackpots are configured is particular to each group, as well as to the machines that are part of that group.

The other types of links are called "mystery links," which typically offer three levels of progressives that can be won at any time. Entry into them is not predicated on your hitting any specified number of symbols, or combinations. Entry into these jackpots can be awarded at random, and that's why they are called "mystery" jackpots. Simply put, you just never know when the game will decide to award you an entry into one of these jackpot features. As long as you are one of the players playing on the machines in that particular group, and you are wagering the required number of credits, you will always be eligible to win any of these jackpots at any time, completely at random.

Why is it a good idea to play on these progressives? Because you are always in the running to win all of the small jackpots, as well as all of the higher jackpots. Some of these also offer the ante bet, or an extra bonus bet, which allows you to play these games for even additional jackpot opportunities.

Aristocrat's pioneering experience in *Hyperlink®* technology began in the 1990s with the introduction of the *Hyperlink®* system, and continues today with an array of progressive options that players everywhere find so very appealing. In 1995, the debut of the *Hyperlink®* theme, *Born to be Wild™*, was first installed in Queensland, Australia and later became a success across the rest of the world. Other *Hyperlink®* games, including *Cash Express®* and *Jackpot Carnival®*, enabled Aristocrat to fill a new high demand because players everywhere liked these new games and chances at great jackpots.

Continued development in the *Hyperlink®* category in the late 1990s and early 2000s led to a greater variety of similar linked games. With the introduction of the *MKVI™* platform, new innovations and levels of player interactivity were achieved via the use of bonus features, touch screen monitors, and the introduction of LCD displays in the top box to show themed graphics and jackpot increments. With the launch of the *VIRIDIAN*™ cabinet on the *GEN7*™ platform in 2008, the next generation of *Hyperlink*® games emerged. Aristocrat has been continually working on their link strategy since the early 1990s, and with the capabilities of the new *GEN7*™ platform, combined with Aristocrat's focus on staying abreast of technology, the future of new linked games is well underway. There will be more of these games available in the future. I begin with *Cash Express*®, the game that started it all.

Cash Express®

Cash Express® was one of Aristocrat's first *Hyperlink*® products. A longstanding success in the marketplace, it is a fine example of the great performing and lasting products Aristocrat develops.

125 - The *Cash Express*® machines in the *Hyperlink*® group of progressives from Aristocrat

What differentiates *Cash Express*® from other Mystery links is the mystery-triggered second-screen bonus feature. This means that the *Cash Express*® bonus feature can be won at any time dur-

126 - The *Cash Express*® jackpot bonus screen

ing any game. The way this happens is that the Station master sounds his whistle, and that announces the start of the feature. Five spinning reels then appear, and you get to choose when to stop each reel spinning. This reveals either a number, or a train symbol. Numbers are added to the jackpot score, while the train symbols reveal higher scoring Bonus Points. After all the reels have stopped, the Bonus Points are added to the total score, and this then determines which of the four available jackpots you have won.

Player's World Super™ is the first multi game pack available under the *Cash Express*® link. As a new way to build on the success of the *Cash Express*® support games, *Player's World Super*™—a new 4-pack multi-game—has now been released. The 4 games were selected to provide a greater choice, and a range of games from which you can choose. The games offered are *5 Dragons*® (a 25-credit *Reel Power*® game), *Turtle Treasure*® (a 25-line game), *Where's the Gold*® (a 25-line game), and *Tiki Torch*® (also a 25-line game). Of course, the benefits to you are many, because you can not only choose from a selection of these games without having to get up and look for them elsewhere in the casino, but you can also play all of these *Cash Express*® games at the same time simply by switching from one game to the other as you want. All of these games also offer separate bonus features and other additional game and pay options. I have already described most of these games elsewhere in this book, but here is a short recap of these games and the bonuses they offer—in addition to, of course, all of the *Hyperlink*® game options and jackpots.

5 Dragons®, a *Reel Power*® 25-credits Game

In this game, the bonus features offer you a selection from the menu of free games choices. This means you can pick your own free game feature as well as the multiplier.

Where's the Gold®—25-Line Game

Here the second screen feature offers you 3 to 10 Free Games and substitute symbols.

Turtle Treasure®—25-Line Game

On this particular version of the *Cash Express®* game, the bonus offers you 10 Free Games.

Tiki Torch®—25-Line Game

This is one of the great games that have been around for quite some time, and, as I mentioned earlier, is among my personal favorites. The bonus feature here offers you 8 Free Games.

Millioni$er®

Building on the proven success of linked games and *Hyperlink®* technology, Aristocrat has created a game called *Millioni$er®*. *Millioni$er®* was the first Wide Area Progressive from Aristocrat. *Millioni$er's®* patented touch-screen-based second screen feature offers four progressive jackpots, each of which can be won at random at any time during any game. These four-tiered progressives give *Millioni$er®* a higher hit frequency that makes it possible for you to keep playing, and so give yourself even more chances for the ultimate top jackpot. As with all of Aristocrat's progressive links, the *Millioni$er®* games come in a variety of game themes.

127 - The *Millioni$er®* machines in the *Hyperlink®* group of progressives from Aristocrat

128 - The *Millioni\$er*® jackpot bonus screens

Millioni\$er® is such a great idea that the folks at Aristocrat couldn't just sit around and let a great thing stay just great. There was a lot more to *Millioni\$er*® than met the eye, and the great game had to get even better. But how do you improve on something which is already so terrific? Well, how about making it bigger? More games? Bigger bonuses? Bigger jackpots? All that makes perfect sense. As a result, a new group of *Hyperlink*® games were developed and—naturally—the best name for it was *Mega Millioni\$er*®. Appropriate, wouldn't you say? Good games deserve better treatment, and great games deserve great treatment. And that's what happened when *Mega Millioni\$er*® became a reality. And here it is, the game next on our agenda.

Mega Millioni\$er®

Quick: Name all the penny slots that have a life-changing, multi-million-dollar jackpot. No? Well, now there *is* one! The *Mega Millioni\$er*® link from Aristocrat is a multi-site progressive that offers higher awards and a life-changing top jackpot. Housed in both the *VIRIDIAN*™ and *RFX*™ cabinets, *Mega Millioni\$er*® looks amazing and performs as incredibly as it looks. Adding an extra layer of fun and excitement, the *Mega Millioni\$er*® base games now include *Player's World Deluxe*™ pack for multi game video slots as well as many other single-title games such as *Geisha*®, *50 Lions*®

and a few new games like *Polynesian Pearl®* and *African Storm®*. It is also available in the very popular *Sun & Moon®* and *Pompeii®* versions for the *RFX™* stepper—which are really great looking, and play even better! I will tell you more about these "steppers" later in this book.

129 - The *Mega Millioni$er®* machines in the *Hyperlink®* group of progressives from Aristocrat

130 - An example of the *Mega Millioni$er®* jackpot values in Nevada

In many jurisdictions, *Mega Millioni$er®* is a multi-site progressive, meaning the progressive jackpot grows from play in different casinos—sometimes even among many casinos in different states (as permitted by the regulatory authorities of those jurisdictions). The game offers higher top awards, and a life-changing multi-million dollar top jackpot on what is usually a penny slot.

Hyperlink® Progressive

131 - The *Mega Millioni$er®* "Choose the Coins" jackpot bonus screens

The *Hyperlink®* Jackpot Feature can be won at random during any bought game. In the bonus, 10 gold coins will appear on the screen, and you are then asked to choose coins until a 3-of-a-kind match is made, at which point you win one of four progressive jackpots. To be able to win the Grand Jackpot you need to be playing with the max bet.

Beat the Bandits®

Mosey on over to my corral, pardner. I hear Madam Red a-callin', and my six-shooter is a itchin'. So, you don't like my spittoon? Well, I'm just gonna have to get you down on your knees and polish it. 'Cause I'm the roughest, tumbliest ole outlaw in these here parts! Ya hear? And don't forget it! Well, that's about as much "movie speak" as I can muster. I may have illusions of being a cowboy, but in my case it's urban cowboy (and no, not the movie). My western exploits are limited to the casinos of the West, and my "six shooter" refers to the number of credits I put in my slot machine. And that, of course, is the perfect segue to the reason for this exploit—which is *Beat the Bandits*®, a great new slot machine game from Aristocrat.

132 - Madam Red in the *Beat the Bandits*® game from Aristocrat

Here we have a slew of villains and heroes, Madam Red, and great shoot 'em ups along with bountiful bonuses. *Beat the Bandits*® is a 30-credits game, where the *Beat the Bandits*® bonus features can be triggered at the end of any bought game. During the *Beat the Bandits*® feature you and Madam Red roll 2 dice each. Add your dice rolls together to reveal your score. A prize is awarded if you or Madam Red rolls a double, or if your score is equal to or greater than Madam Red's score. The prize won depends upon your roll, and only the highest prize award is paid.

If you or Madam Red roll a double, then you win the choice of playing the GRANNY, BANDITO or GAMBLER jackpot bonus feature. If neither Madam

133 - The Dice Roll Bonus screen in the Madam Red bonus for the *Beat the Bandits*® game

Red nor you roll a double, and Madam Red's score is greater than your score, then a prize of between $1.50 and $5.00 is awarded, and the Granny, Bandito and Gambler jackpot amounts are each increased by $1.00.

The three linked progressive jackpots are named Gambler, Bandito and Granny. Once you enter this bonus round, you are asked to choose which of the three jackpots you wish to

134 - Choose the jackpot you want to play in the *Beat the Bandits*® Bonus

play. It is best to look at the values of each of the jackpots to decide which one to play. Here are the three bonus games, their seed amounts, and the average amounts at which the bonuses are won.

Granny Game Bonus

The jackpot on this game starts at $14.70, and the average amount reached when this jackpot is won is about $20. During this bonus, you and Granny have 5 shots each to shoot at bottles or cans. Touch a bottle or can to shoot it. Your score is equal

135 - The Granny Game Bonus screen in the *Beat the Bandits*® game

to the number of bottles or cans that you hit. Granny's score is equal to the number of bottles or cans that Granny hits. The Granny jackpot is won if your score is equal to or greater than Granny's. The Granny jackpot amount is increased by $16.75 if Granny's score is greater than yours. You have about a 73% chance of winning the Granny Jackpot.

Bandito Game Bonus

In this bonus game the bonus starts at $32.60, and the average amount that you win is usually somewhere around $50. Dur-

136 - The Bandito Bonus screen in the *Beat the Bandits*® game

ing this bonus you are trying to find the Bandito in the jewelry store. There are 12 windows behind which the Bandito may be hiding. You have 4 attempts to find the Bandito, by touching a window to attempt to find the villain. You will win the Bandito jackpot if you find the Bandito. If you do not, the Bandito jackpot amount is increased by about $7. You have about a 33% chance of finding the Bandito and winning this jackpot bonus.

Gambler Game Bonus

In this game, the bonus starts at $100.00, and the average amount you can win by winning this bonus is about $150.00 at the time it is hit. To play this bonus, you are dealt 7 cards from a single 52-card deck. Touch 5 of the 7 cards to reveal your hand. The Gambler has a pair of aces. You beat the Gambler's hand if your hand consists of 2 aces, 2 pairs, 3 or more cards of the same rank, 5 cards of the same suit or a sequence of 5 consecutive cards. The Gambler jackpot is won if you beat the Gambler's hand. If you don't, the Gambler jackpot amount is then increased by $4.89. You have about an 11% chance of winning the gambler jackpot bonus.

137 - The Gambler Bonus screen in the *Beat the Bandits*® game

Mystery Jackpot

In addition to all the other bonuses and game plays, there is also the Mystery jackpot, which can be won at the end of any bought game.

138 - The Mystery Jackpot Bonus screen in the *Beat the Bandits*® game

There are two games under the *Beat the Bandits*® theme: *Jungle Joe*™ and *Fortune Princess*™. Each of these games has its own base game features, which I will now take you through.

Jungle Joe™

Most people don't know that the original book "Tarzan of the Apes" was written by author Edgar Rice Burroughs in the early parts of the 20th century on cocktail napkins in nightclubs. Not only that, since Mr. Burroughs had never been outside of the United States, he was not aware that Africa did not have any tigers, and so the original Tarzan book was populated by Bengal tigers which belonged more to India than to Africa. Most people also don't know that the movie "Tarzan" was first filmed as a silent movie in 1917. The star of that movie was the first ever motion picture Tarzan—and his name was Elmo Lincoln. Put that in your napkin, and pull it out at trivia time at your next party and you're bound to score a winner.

But as the talkies came, the movies needed a new, muscular Tarzan—and one who could act. Lo and behold, there came the persona of Mr. Johnny Weissmuller, and the rest, as they say, is history. When his career in the motion pictures was over in the 1950s, he moved over to television and starred in a series called "Jungle Jim." He was kind of like a grown-up Tarzan in a safari outfit toting an elephant gun and a chimp around the jungles of Africa. It was a pretty good TV show for the time, and I remember watching it as a little boy and being enthralled by it. And that's why this new slot machine game reminds me of that story.

In *Jungle Joe*™, you can win 10, 15, or 20 free games with 3, 4 or 5 PYRAMID symbols respectively. All wins during the free games are multiplied by 2, 3 or 5. This bonus feature can be triggered again during the bonus rounds. The bet per reel and reels played are the same as the game that triggered the feature.

Fortune Princess™

Similarly, in the *Fortune Princess*™ game you can win 15 free games with 3, 4 or 5 scattered PEARL symbols. During the free games, if one or more LADY symbols substitute in a win, then the pay for that win is multiplied by 5, 10 or 15. All other wins during the free games are tripled. This bonus feature can be triggered again while in the bonus rounds. The bet multiplier and lines played are the same as the game that triggered the feature.

Beijing Bonanza™

139 - The *Beijing Bonanza*™ community game from Aristocrat

Beijing Bonanza™ is based on the *Lucky 88*® game I mentioned earlier. It is Aristocrat's first community and tournament style game. Community gaming means that everyone on a bank works together to win mutual prizes. Tournament gaming means everyone on the bank competes against each other to win the prizes. If you enjoy playing community style games, then this terrific game should be part of your selection.

The game is a bonus bet game, with a 25+15 credit bet requirement, for a total minimum wager of 40 credits. This will give you the opportunity to unlock all of the bonuses and community game features available in this game. Each machine in the group of community games has its own distinct identity, either in the form of a fortune animal or a sign of the zodiac. The *Beijing Bonanza*™ bonus feature can be triggered at any time completely at random, and is usually time-based, meaning it will trigger on average about every 10 minutes. This is only an average, because the feature trigger is completely random, and therefore cannot be specifically predicted.

Beijing Bonanza™ Community Feature

Once the Community feature is triggered, one of the machines will be randomly selected to choose the feature. All the other machines will then play the same chosen feature. The feature will include either free games with a multiplier or the Dice Feature. Each machine has its own multiplier, and the *Beijing Bonanza*™ multiplier value is a function of the bet and time. The community game win values are multiplied by *Beijing Bonanza*™ multiplier.

Beijing Bonanza™ Tournament Feature

The Tournament feature is triggered at random. All machines (including non played machines) will enter the Tournament mode. The tournament feature is a race to collect your Zodiac symbols and fill the pyramid. The tournament will be completed when one of the machines fills its pyramid with zodiac symbols. When the machine is ranked first, the screen color changes to purple. Prizes are won for placing 1st, 2nd, 3rd and 4th. The prize will be multiplied by your personal multiplier.

And that's how you get to play not only a series of great games, each with its own individual bonuses and pays, but also the variety of community features available within the *Beijing Bonanza*™ group of games.

The most exciting progressive on today's casino floor is a mystery—an *Xtreme Mystery®* from Aristocrat. *Xtreme Mystery®* progressives can be added to any *GEN7*™ standard or premium Aristocrat base games. These signage packages can be added to banks of machines ranging in number from as few as six to as many as 100. *Xtreme Mystery®* jackpots continuously add to player excitement because the three-level jackpot can be won at any time during any bought game. What's

140 - The *Xtreme Mystery®* Bonus *Bank* machines from Aristocrat

more, *Xtreme Mystery®* jackpots can be won with any credit bet and with any number of lines played.

Xtreme Mystery® is available on several great themes including *Golden Pyramids®*, *Golden Challenge®*, *Inca Fortune®*, *Sky Heroes*™, *Island Delight®*, *Hollywood Dreams®* and *Prosperity®*.

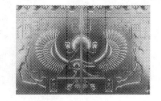

Look for these themed banks the next time you visit your favorite casino, and keep your eyes open for new titles as they are made available.

13

Reel Slots—Steppers

In the gaming industry, the word "stepper" refers to a slot machine that has a more "traditional" look, feel and appeal. These are the kinds of machines with which most of us are familiar from the historic casinos—games that have a handle to pull and spinning reels that look like a barrel. Many of these machines can still be found in the modern casino, and they are as popular today as they were in years past.

These "stepper" machines are traditionally available in the 3-reel and 5-reel formats, simply meaning that there are either 3 reels or 5 reels on those particular games. They are easy to spot, and I'm certain you will understand the difference as soon as you see one, as opposed to all of the other machines, such as the video games. Because technology now allows the combination of reel games that also incorporate numerous video features, such as top box and touchscreen technology, these traditional reel machines have become anything but "traditional." In the modern casinos of the 21ˢᵗ century these stepper machines offer LCD technology that permits a variety of bonusing rounds, as well as opportunities for *Reel Power*® games, *Triple Standalone Progressives*, bonus bets and *Xtra Reel Power*™ spins.

The Aristocrat stepper product is called *RFX*™, which stands for "Reel Effects," meaning that Aristocrat developed intelligent reel hardware that resulted in fine-grained reel control and consistently reliable performance. The *VIRIDIAN RFX*™ stepper uses new and more reliable reels co-developed with the leading industry reel manufacturer Gamesman. These specially designed reels were crafted to eliminate "bounce" and visual fatigue, so you can play longer and in greater comfort.

All of these capabilities have made playing stepper games just as entertaining as the video games, and in many ways additionally exciting to play. In this chapter, I will show you several of the best games now available, beginning with the kind of bull ride that any top Rodeo would be proud to host—a game called: *Big Ride*™.

Big Ride™

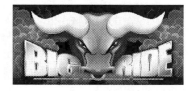

This slot machine game from Aristocrat reminds me of one of the first mechanical bulls that became extremely famous in several motion pictures. It happened to be installed at Gilley's in Dallas, Texas. This mechanical bull would romp and snort while he twisted and bucked, throwing drunken cowboys all over the place. Cowgirls, too. It was a rip-roaring raunching time with cowboys in boots and cowboy hats, and never-ending flowing beer. And indeed so it was here in Las Vegas. That's how I see this game whenever I play it. It has the snorting bull and cowboy hats, boots, cowbells, and a lot of other paraphernalia that leads me back to the land of youth where I once looked mighty handsome in my boots and cowboy hat. There is definitely no "bull" about this game.

141 - The *Big Ride*™ *Reel Power*® slot machine from Aristocrat

Big Ride™ is a 25-credit *Reel Power*® game, and a new addition to the *VIRIDIAN RFX Stepper*™ library. All wins begin with outer reels and pay left to right, anywhere on adjacent reels. The WILD BULL symbol substitutes for all symbols—*including* scattered RED BULL symbols. Choose your number of reels, then choose your bet per reel to begin the game.

Big Ride™ Free Games Bonus

You can win up to 15 free games with 3 scattered RED BULL symbols. You will then be asked to choose your 8-second Challenge Feature, based on the number of TIMERS symbols you expect to collect. The higher the number of TIMERS, the higher the reward. All TIMERS symbols appearing anywhere are counted in each free spin. If you achieve the minimum TIMERS symbols selected in the challenge screen, the corresponding bonus is added after the spins. During the free games, any win with a WILD BULL substituting is multiplied by 2, 3 or 5. Free games can be won again dur-

142 - The *Big Ride*™ Free Games bonus screens

ing the feature under the original challenge selection. Reels selected and the bet multiplier are the same as the initiating game.

Hillbillions™

This is another one of those games that absolutely cracks me up. Once you start playing it, and hitting some of the pays, you will never forget it. It is a terrific game, and available in low denomination for greater fun and longevity. You will always know you are playing this game whenever you get the little hillbilly fella yelp-

ing "YeeeHaaaa," and whistling at you. I don't know why—perhaps it's just me—but I break out laughing every time one of those little fellas does that. The game itself is a 20-line + 10-Credit ante bet game, with 3 bonus features, plus the progressive jackpot feature.

In order to be eligible for all the jackpots and the bonus features, you must wager the additional 10-credits bonus bet in addition to the minimum bet requirement. This makes the game a minimum of 30 credits game, in order to be eligible for all of features and bonuses.

143 - The hilarious *Hillbillions*™ reel slot machine from Aristocrat

Any one of the major, minor or mini jackpots can be won at any time when the Gold Panning feature is initiated (also at random). In the feature you pan for gold nuggets. You will be given 5 picks, with which to collect NUGGETS symbols. Each pick contains 1 to 5 NUGGETS, or a credit prize, or 5 extra picks. The level of the prize won is determined by the number of NUGGETS collected. The jackpot prizes are based on the following number of NUGGETS collected:

- 29 or more Nuggets collected wins the Major jackpot
- 21 to 28 Nuggets collected wins the Minor jackpot
- 10 to 20 Nuggets collected wins the Mini jackpot
- 9 or less Nuggets collected wins a consolation prize of 400 Credits

144 - The *Hillbillions*™ Gold Panning Bonus game screen

145 - The *Hillbillions*™ progressive jackpot and game screens

In addition to these progressive jackpots, the game also offers three additional bonuses.

Log Roll Bonus

You have 3 chances to choose which Hillbilly can stay on the log. An award pointer moves up the prize ladder each time the player-selected Hillbilly wins the log roll contest.

146 - The *Hillbillions*™ Log Roll Bonus game screen

Going Fishin' Bonus

The Hillbilly fishes twice for prizes. The prizes caught meter will indicate the value of the prizes caught. You can then choose to collect the win, or continue to fish to win more prizes. If you choose to continue, but the boat sinks, half of the prizes won up to that point are awarded, and the feature ends.

147 - The *Hillbillions*™ Going Fishin' Bonus game screen

Free Games Bonus

You can win up to 10 free games. All winning combinations with a HILLBILLY substituting are multiplied by 2, 3, 5 or 10, as indicated.

148 - The *Hillbillions*™ Free Games Bonus game screens

It's enough to make you want to pack your trailer and head for them thar hills. Ain't that right, cousin? You don't mind me callin' you cousin, now do ya? Why, all the folks in these here parts are my cousins. So I guess you's one of 'em. Heehaw!

King Cobra™

Ever thought of trying to charm a snake? No, I don't mean the kind that comes to your door and tries to sell you something. I mean the kind that you find in India, where the fakir plays the flute and the cobra rises up from the basket. Did you ever wonder what makes the snake rise up in this way and then sway back and forth as the fakir plays the flute? Well, it has absolutely nothing to do with the flute, or the sounds it makes, because the snake can't hear. What makes the snake do this is a natural reaction to the motion of the flute. That's why the fakir moves the flute back and forth and up and down, creating movements that the snake perceives as potentially dangerous. That's why it comes out of the basket and rears up, flaying its neck in that distinctive cobra look.

Additionally, the flute that the fakir uses looks to the snake like some other snake or predator, but the snake is not sure whether it is something that will strike at it, or something that *it* should strike *at*. And that's why the snake is continually weaving back and forth, following the motions of the flute. It is waiting to find out if this is somehow a threat to it. It all makes for a great show, but you don't really need to listen to that screeching flute, because the sound of it has absolutely nothing to do with the magic of this performance.

All of this aside, here we are dealing with a great new slot machine that uses the *King Cobra*™ as a theme, offering a variety of pays and bonuses. All wins begin with the leftmost reel and pay left to right only on adjacent reels, except scatters.

149 - The *King Cobra*™ reel slot machine from Aristocrat

King Cobra™ Free Games Bonus

In the *King Cobra*™ Bonus you can win from 3 to 10 free games and 1 to 3 Wild Bite Symbols. The *King Cobra*™ Feature is triggered when 3, 4 or 5 scattered Snake Charmer symbols appear. You are then asked to touch a basket to charm the *King Cobra*™ and reveal the number of free games you have won, and then select a snake charmer to reveal what symbols become wild for the free games. Symbols that you win change to red and become wild during the free games.

150 - The *King Cobra*™ bonus screen

151 - The *King Cobra*™ Snake Charmer Bonus screen

Additional free games are awarded when 3, 4 or 5 scattered Snake Charmers symbols appear in the window, in any position, and will be played with the same number of free spins and the same wild symbols that were chosen in the *King Cobra*™ Feature selection screen. Credits bet and lines played are the same as the game that triggered the feature.

152 - The *King Cobra*™ main game and bonus screen

So now you can take a bite out of the snake, instead of the other way around. No more worried looks around the room to see where the snake might be. It's on *King Cobra*™, this great new game from Aristocrat.

Salmon Rapids™

Among my favorite TV shows are those nature specials where you watch bears fish for Salmon during the salmon runs on the great rivers. Some of the bears are quite good at this, while others stumble around as the slippery fish get away from them time and time again. It's particularly funny when the bear cubs try this for the first time, chasing the salmon all over and getting nowhere. These nature specials are interesting, cute, funny and joyful all at the same time—just like this slot machine. *Salmon Rapids*™ gives you the chance to catch the salmon bonuses which may give you big credits and wins.

What if there were 1,024 ways for you to win? Would you play longer? Have more fun? Keep coming back for more? Now Aristocrat has created *XRP RFX*™—an *RFX*™ stepper with *Xtra Reel Power*™. The *XRP RFX*™ is a totally new game category whose unique combination gives you up to 1,024 ways to win with every spin. A 40-credit minimum bet covers all reels, and this unlocks all of the wins and bonuses. If you are already famil-iar with *Xtra Reel Power*™ games, you are well on the way to understanding what this new concept means and how it can benefit your play.

153 - The *Salmon Rapids*™ slot machine from Aristocrat

Salmon Rapids™ is an *Xtra Reel Power*™ game, where all wins are paid left to right, except the scattered Fisherman symbols. The Salmon symbols substitute for all other symbols, except scatters. The Salmon symbols appear on reels 2, 3 and 4 only.

Free Games Bonus

154 - The *Salmon Rapids*™ Free Games Bonus screen

The 3, 4 or 5 scattered Fisherman symbols win 10, 15 or 20 free games respec-tively. During the free games, each Salmon symbol that appears anywhere on reels 2, 3 or 4 will multiply the total win for that spin by either 2x or 3x. If more than one Salmon occurs, the multipliers are applied successively up to 27x total. In addition, 5 extra free games will be awarded if any 2 scatters occur during any free game.

Old Bayou™

This is also an *Xtra Reel Power*™ game, and as with *Salmon Rapids*™, all wins pay left to right, except for the scattered Dragon Fly symbols. The Water Lilly symbol substitutes for all symbols, except for the scatters. The Water Lilly symbols appear on reels 2, 3 and 4 only. When you hit 3, 4 or 5 scattered Dragon Fly symbols, you will win 10, 15 or 20 free games respectively. During the free games, each Water Lilly symbol that appears anywhere on reels 2, 3 or 4 will multiply the total win for that spin by either 2x or 3x. If more than one Water Lilly symbol occurs, the multipliers are applied successively up to 27x total.

155 - The *Old Bayou*™ slot machine from Aristocrat

So if you take a trip on *Old Bayou*™, watch out the for Crocks! And, while you're at it, be sure to collect all the winnings. After all, why not enjoy some Gumbo cash while you're at it, right?

OASIS 360™ Gaming Systems

W e have reached a point in this book where it is appropriate to talk a little bit about the operating system that links the machines on casino floors containing the slot machines that I have described so far. This operating system is called *OASIS 360*™, and it is a bit like the network that runs all the computers inside the slot machines—except this is not an "operating system" in the same sense that, for example, Windows XP is for your personal PC. *OASIS 360*™ does not run the software inside each machine, because that is the game software which is part of the operating system for that particular machine, and its self-contained game, or games. The only other kind of networked operating system on the casino floor that will be similar to that which operates a personal computer is called SBG, which stands for "Server-Based Gaming," a method of delivering game content to the casino floor without each game necessarily being contained within the machine's cabinet.

    OASIS 360™ is an integrated system that provides a variety of solutions to the casino operator. It is directed primarily at providing a real-time player interface, meaning a real-time bridge between you—the player—and the casino, and the casino's on-the-floor staff. Think of this as a means of getting what you want, when *you* want it. *OASIS 360*™ provides not only a constant real-time data stream that tells the casino who is playing, what they are playing, and when they are playing it, but it also provides a means for the casino to inform you—the player—of what they have to offer, such as *Bonus Points*™, comps, special events, invitations, restaurant availability, bonus cash, and a variety of other two-way directional features from which all players can benefit.

A host of opportunities opens up for you as soon as you visit a casino that uses the *OASIS 360*™ Casino management system. The greatest benefit to you—the player—is, of course, the immediacy with which you can get everything you have earned, everything to which you are entitled, and everything the casino has available for you. That is the greatest benefit of *OASIS 360*™, and one of the main reasons you should always sign up for your player's club card at your favorite casino, particularly if you recognize the games I have mentioned in this book and the *OASIS 360*™ player interface system as being available there. If it is not, ask the management *why not*.

OASIS 360™ is a comprehensive gaming solution comprised of configurable operational modules that collect, analyze and report gaming and non-gaming activity, giving operators a 360-degree view of their enterprise. The tools provided by this product suite make for a one-of-a-kind experience for the player. As you enter a casino that has *OASIS 360*™ as its Casino Management System, you will benefit from experience-enhancing characteristics tied directly to the *OASIS 360*™ product. These small touches let you know that you are in an exciting place, that your favorite casino has gone the extra mile, and your experience will be one to remember. When you step into an *OASIS 360*™ casino you are quickly enrolled in the player's club and receive the card that will afford you specialized privileges, opportunities to win, and much more.

The first thing you notice, after all the wonderful gaming titles, is the highly interactive LCD screen strategically positioned on your favorite slot machines. Through this device you obtain first-hand updates on casino events, promotions, deals on services available at the casino and much more. This LCD is called a *Sentinel III™* and serves not only as the link between the *OASIS 360™* Casino Management System and the slot machines on the casino floor, but more importantly as a valuable resource for connecting with you as a player.

While this technology is the first line of communication from the System to the player, much more than promotion takes place at the *Sentinel III™*. This device also serves as a doorway into your casino account information, which is the *OASIS 360™* cashless wagering solution called *"Personal Banker®." Personal Banker®* allows you to use your player's club card and assigned PIN to electronically transfer cash, points, or promotional credits to and from their accounts and EGM's (Electronic Gaming Machines, which is industry language for "slots"). While the functionality may be uniform, the look and feel of this solution will vary depending on the customization for each gaming property using it. As a customizable solution, the *SpeedMedia®* product (the bonusing engine which controls media on the S III) offers skinning. This "skinning" allows your favorite casino to brand *Sentinel III™* displays according to themes with which you are familiar. The Skinning capability is especially evident when you use your *Personal Banker®* account. So whether it is *"Loco Loot®"* or *"Flash Cash™"* you feel right at home because of the familiar look and feel of your account option screens. This is similar to going to your favorite super market or web page: You know where everything is because it is familiar and you've been there before.

Once you've checked your balance, downloaded points and observed all of the exciting updates streaming across the interactive screen, you begin playing. You'll then find that there is more in store from the *Sentinel III™* device, such as "bonusing." Consider Bonusing as extra chances to win or a gift made available to you just for playing. An example of Bonusing offered by *OASIS 360™* properties is a velocity-based bonus known as *Splashdown Countdown™*. Think of this as a reward for betting as fast as you can within a given time period, maybe two minutes. Bet as fast as you can and earn as little as 20 points or as much as 500 points. Its up to you and doubles your chance to win.

Another type of promotion you may see in an *OASIS 360*™ casino is the mystery style bonusing promotion or *Ricochet Rewards*™. This is a promotion that can hit at anytime and also rewards other carded players just for being there. A good example of this would be your favorite casino randomly showering players with money once they bet enough at a slot machine. If you were sitting next to a person who received such an award, you would catch a little money too, right? Same concept, except in order to get close enough to catch some cash you just have to have your card in your favorite machine. Whether you are the person getting showered with money or points, or the person randomly selected, you are a winner anytime when you are a member of the player's club at an *OASIS 360*™ casino.

These Bonusing capabilities are controlled by *SpeedMedia*®, and deployed to the *Sentinel III*™ device that makes your experience exciting while expanding the opportunities to win and enriching every moment at any *OASIS 360*™ casino.

Announcements are another key contributor to your pleasure at your favorite *OASIS 360*™ casino. Through the *Sentinel III*™ all players are informed of the undeniable fact that patrons are winning at this casino, through solutions like *Totalizer*™, which tells you how much the casino has given away with *SpeedMedia*® promotions over a set period of time, and *Jackpot Announcer*™, a solution that announces Jackpots to every machine in the casino as soon as they are triggered.

Content Delivery Manager™ is another innovation that takes variety to a new level by creating endless possibilities in terms of what games, advertisements, specials, and media in general are displayed on the *Sentinel III*™. Think of this as the same type of functionality used to create those new Apps. Anyone can develop an App and you have the opportunity to buy it. The casino can, therefore, develop any type of promotion, drawing, or a way to play and you get to trigger them by playing your favorite game.

As you can see, the *OASIS 360*™ brings a great deal directly to the slot machine when it comes to reaching you, the player— but it doesn't stop with just these products. This brief introduction is just a window into the patron's experience when playing at a casino that has the *OASIS 360*™ product, and these descriptions do not include all products offered by the Aristocrat products suite. For that, we now showcase the reasons why players—and operators—both benefit from the installation of *OASIS 360*™.

Sentinel III™ Assembly

The *Sentinel*® unit is the first link between the gaming machine and the *OASIS 360*™ System. In order to communicate with the *OASIS 360*™ System, each electronic gaming machine (EGM) has a *Sentinel III*™ assembly mounted inside it. The *Sentinel III*™ assembly consists of a *Sentinel*® communication board and appropriate cabling to connect the assembly to the specific machine type.

156 - *OASIS 360*™ *Sentinel III*™ interface

Sentinel®

The *Sentinel III*™ unit monitors and transmits signals from a single EGM to the *OASIS 360*™ System. It also transmits signals to and from the card reader assembly attached to the EGM. The card reader and display plug into the *Sentinel*® board. The *Sentinel*® unit monitors what happens at the EGM and sends this information to the *OASIS 360*™ System.

Sentinel III™ Features

- Located inside each Class III EGM, *Sentinel III*™ monitors multiple signals from a single EGM
- *Sentinel III*™ provides the first link between a gaming machine and the *OASIS 360*™ System
- Interfaces between card readers and the *OASIS 360*™ System
- Stores transactions in Non-Volatile Memory as a safeguard in case of power outage
- 10/100 Ethernet connection provides cost effective wiring and faster network response
- Non-volatile storage capability for video clips, graphics and program functionality
- Touch-screen menus provide quicker user input and intuitive menu navigation
- Player-related information is displayed on the touch screen LCD
- Integrated stereophonic audio system with speakers
- Scriptable animation and movie support offering enhanced visual display capabilities and options
- Downloadable code updates and multimedia content updates

Personal Banker®

The patented *Personal Banker*® module allows players to use their player's club card and assigned PIN (Personal Identification Number) to electronically transfer cash, points, or promotional credits to and from their accounts and EGMs. All funds are stored at the system database level, not on the player's club card. *Personal Banker*® is an optional, purchased component of the *OASIS 360*™ System that provides additional functionality and options to *Super-PlayMate*™ and *BlackBart Prime*®. Players must have a club account, players card, and PIN to conduct *Personal Banker*® transactions at an EGM. Gaming jurisdiction regulations determine where this option is available.

157 - *Personal Banker®* interface

Players can use *Personal Banker®* to:

- Transfer (upload) cashable EGM credits to their players club account.
- Transfer (download) PBT cash from their account to the EGM credit meter.
- Redeem earned slot club points and transfer (download) converted cash or promo dollar equivalents to the EGM credit meter.
- Transfer (download) PBT promo dollars to the EGM credit meter.
- View points, cash, and promo balances on demand by using the card reader attached to the EGM.

Required *OASIS 360™* Applications

- *Administrator™* - Controls access to menu items and other features
- *Super-PlayMate™* - Player tracking component of the Oasis 360™ System
- *BlackBart Prime®* - Tracks machine accounting information

SpeedMedia® Administrator™

SpeedMedia® provides the tools for preparing and customizing content files containing multimedia promotions displayed on the *Sentinel III™ SpeedMedia®* promotions generate enthusiasm and provide innovative ways for casinos to reward loyalty and develop recurring and repeatable revenue. This excitement is generated through a variety of new and exciting games for patrons, in addition to standard slot play. *SpeedMedia®* is a 32-bit application designed to run within the Microsoft Windows® XP Professional operating system.

158 - *SpeedMedia®* Scheduling Calendar

Features of *SpeedMedia® Administrator*™

- Advanced technology attracts players to gaming products
- Maintains excitement and rewards patron loyalty
- Patron media and promotion content is automatically delivered to key games on the casino floor
- Provides player recognition through targeted messages for special player events, such as birthdays and anniversaries
- Supports video with sound and still images using common file formats
- Storyboard Editor facilitates inserting, moving or removing images and video with audio. Create a script for each *Sentinel III*™ and preview the script
- Associates multimedia files with promotional and campaign events that are automatically downloaded to *Sentinel III*™-equipped games
- Provides a flexible and structured framework that Aristocrat and third-party vendors can use to deliver interactive *Adobe Flash®*-based content to *Sentinel III*™ devices
- Default content media ensures continuous *Sentinel III*™ content display

- Event calendar provides immediate visibility for current and future promotional events and campaigns scheduled at the casino
- Reports are available to assist in analyzing the effectiveness of promotions and to provide historical data. Ensures compliance with regulatory requirements.

Skinning

As a customizable solution, the *SpeedMedia®* product (the bonusing engine which controls media on the S III) offers skinning. Skinning allows operators to brand *Sentinel III™* displays according to their current branding strategy. The Skinning capability is especially evident when the player is using their *Personal Banker®* account. So, whether it is *"Looney Loot™"* or *"Flash™,"* players feel at home because of the familiar look and feel of their account option screens.

Jackpot Announcement™

Jackpot Announcements™ are custom messages set up in *SpeedMedia® Administrator™*. A *Jackpot Announcement™* is displayed on one or more *Sentinel III™s* when a player hits a jackpot over a predetermined amount. *Jackpot Announcement™* can be targeted to a specific set of players (both carded and non-carded) and/or machines. Each *Jackpot Announcement™* event has two separate options to configure multimedia and customized message for carded and non-carded players.

159 - The *Jackpot Announcement™* screen

Totalizer Announcements™

Totalizer Announcements™ is a module that displays a running total of awards given over a defined period for *Splashdown Countdown*™, *Ricochet Rewards*™ or both applications. *Totalizer Announcements*™ can be tailored to eligible players, eligible EGMs, and during a selected time frame. Each *Totalizer Announcement*™ has the following features:

- Media content
- Custom Message options
- Trigger criteria
- Player eligibility criteria
- Machine eligibility criteria
- Schedule criteria

160 - The *Totalizer*™ screen example

When a *Totalizer Announcement*™ occurs, the selected message and media associated with that event is displayed on the *Sentinel III*™ device.

Bonus Points™

The *Bonus Points*™ module is used to create and schedule special casino *Bonus Points*™ promotion events. The *Bonus Points*™ events can be used to attract players to the casino or to reward higher denomination players. There are two main types of bonus events:

- Events based upon frequency, and
- Multiplier events

Frequency events award a specified number of *Bonus Points*™ each time something significant happens. For example, 1,000 *Bonus Points*™ might be awarded once per year to players who visit within 30 days of their birthday or anniversary date.

Multiplier events award points during a specified period. For example, double points might be offered on St. Patrick's Day, or triple points might be offered between 6:00 and 9:00 PM EST. Monday evening hours during *Monday Night Football*®, and so on—whatever the operator may wish to include.

Features of *Bonus Points*™

- Multiplier - Multiplies earned points up to 100 times
- Frequency - Per day, per play, per week, per month and/or per year
- Player Enrollment - Includes player interests, player groups and/or all players
- Date - The associated rewards for a plus or minus specified number of days around an event, calendar week or calendar month. Examples include anniversary date, birth date and entry date (enrollment date)
- Event Scheduler - Allows the user to select date and time ranges in the provided calendar windows
- Machine Groups - Criteria available for each group includes machine number range, type ID range, denomination, casino, section, area, and location

Splashdown Countdown™

Splashdown Countdown™ is a promotional event setup in *SpeedMedia*® *Administrator*™. The primary objective of the *Splashdown Countdown*™ promotion is to encourage players to keep playing with the anticipation of winning a promotion award. A timer is activated when an eligible player playing on an eligible machine meets a *Splashdown Countdown*™ trigger threshold. While the timer is active, if an eligible player meets a countdown winner trigger threshold that player receives a *Splashdown Countdown*™ award.

The trigger values can be configured to accumulate by an individual player or by a group of players playing on eligible machines. Each *Splashdown Countdown*™ promotion has four multimedia events (Countdown Trigger, Celebration, Winner Finale, and Finale) associated with it. Casino operators have an option to use either custom multimedia or the default graphics provided with each *Sentinel III*™ unit.

161 - The *Splashdown Countdown*™ player screen interface

Ricochet Rewards™

Ricochet Rewards™ is a promotional event setup in *SpeedMedia*® *Administrator*™. It is activated when an eligible player begins playing on an eligible machine and meets the promotion trigger threshold. During the event a predefined number of randomly selected players receive the promotion award. With each random player selection, the program selects a prize from a predetermined set of awards and then selects an amount between a minimum and maximum amount per prize. These actions, all randomly selected, keep occurring until the set amount of ricochets or the set end date/time has been reached. Trigger values can be

162 - The *Ricochet Rewards*™ player screen interface

configured to accumulate by an individual player, or by a group of players playing on eligible machines. Each *Ricochet Rewards*™ promotion has two multimedia events (Trigger and Celebration) associated with it. Casino operators have an option to use custom multimedia or the default graphics provided with each *Sentinel III*™ unit.

Super-PlayMate™

Super-PlayMate™ is the player tracking component of the *OASIS 360*™ System and provides casino marketing personnel with various information tools for managing and analyzing important player and group information. *Super-PlayMate*™ enables casinos to track, promote, and reward player gaming activity. Players earn points and comp dollars based on actual slot and pit game play. Casino-defined formulas determine how much game play is required for a player to accumulate points and/or comp dollars. *Super-PlayMate*™ tracks points and comp dollars as they are earned and redeemed. Players may also be awarded *Bonus Points*™ for promotions using the *Bonus Points*™ Promotions program.

Content Delivery Manager™

The *Content Delivery Manager*™ (CDM) is a feature of *Speed-Media*® that delivers Adobe® Flash®-based program files to *Sentinel III*™ devices. *SpeedMedia*® *Content Delivery Manager*™ allows interactive content created and managed by Aristocrat or Third-Party vendors to be downloaded to run on *Sentinel III*™ devices. These flash program files display on *Sentinel III*™ devices and are based on a configured schedule with a variety of pre-defined triggers. Since the multimedia content downloaded through the CDM is prepared and managed by programs outside of *SpeedMedia*® Administrator™, *SpeedMedia*® Administrator™ can be used only for viewing and monitoring CDM events.

Okay, if by now you have a headache, take two aspirin and head immediately to your favorite casino for a little one-on-one with some of the machines I have profiled in this book. I wanted you to know not only what goes into the machines themselves, but also into the integrated network solutions that together facilitate all of those features that are now available in the casinos of the 21st century on all of the games that I have described in this book. It is increasingly important that you—as a successful slot player—become aware not only of the new innovations in slot machines themselves, but also of all the bonusing and reward programs that casinos can offer. Because of all this, you can benefit by using the player's club card, and by becoming aware of what systems like *OASIS 360*™ are, and what they do.

It is equally important for you to understand how casinos operate in regard to providing the various incentives, giveaways, and promotions they create on a regular basis and make available to their players. Even if you didn't understand all the information presented in this chapter, you now at least have broader knowledge of what goes into that marketing mailer, or that bonus cash, that your favorite casino sends you, and how it came to be. And, if you are not getting any of these promotions or offers, it is doubly important that you become aware of how these things operate, so that next time you visit your favorite casino you can immediately sign up for the player's club and begin to take advantage of this technology.

Finally, it's important for you to realize, when playing in casinos that offer the *OASIS 360*™ networked player system, that by taking advantage of your player's club card and the bonuses that are thus offered through the use of this system, you can often increase your payback percentage on the slot machines by several percentage points. No, using a player's club card does not alter the actual machine's payback percentage—rather it is the use of your player's club card that generates *additional* benefits that are then *combined together* with a total value of your winnings. Together they translate into an overall higher payback percentage than you would receive had you not played with a player's club card, and thus be able to take advantage of the benefits that the casinos provide for you as a reward for being an *OASIS 360*™ valued player and customer. And now you know this, and it is therefore yet another piece in the armor of knowledge that allows you to gain the greatest reward from your gaming entertainment.

Postscript

People who play slots are usually divided into two groups: those who play slot machines purely as a form of entertainment, and those who play primarily to hit big pays. People who come to casinos are also divided into two groups: those who come to win, and those who simply "hope" to win. Everyone who goes to a casino has high hopes. Some hope to have a great vacation, some hope they will get to see the best shows available, some hope to get a good bargain for a last-minute trip, and just about everyone hopes to win—at least something. There is nothing wrong with being hopeful, but many people combine "hope" with "wishful thinking." Wishful thinking is a condition of hope that afflicts most of us, especially those of us—like me—who tend to be perennial optimists. We hope, and wish really hard, that we will not only have a great time, but that we will also win. When we win, naturally we have a great time, but when we lose, well, that great time isn't all that great. So, what differentiates those players who *always* have a good time from those who only have a good time *sometimes* (and sometimes have to recover from a bad time before they can have a good time again)?

It all has to do with your initial approach to visiting the casino, and playing the slots you have chosen. This is directly related to your ability to acquire some knowledge before you do this. I don't mean that you have to become an expert and study the ins and outs of slot machines, or somehow become a gambling maven. On the contrary, all you really need is some preliminary knowledge—

something that will allow you to know what to look for, and how to play it when you find it. The fact that we human beings have the ability and power of choice is all well and good, as long as we know how to navigate the world of choices and find out which choices are the better ones. As choices apply to slot machines, among the many that are available to you in the modern casino of the 21st century, which of them do you choose? And, once you choose them, do you know what they pay? How they pay? And, most importantly, how to play?

The answers to these, and many other questions and choices, are in this book. I have provided you with a cross-section of what are universally considered some of the best slot machines and games now available in modern casinos everywhere. With this book in hand, you have a guide that you can use to navigate those many choices, and to select those games that you decide to play *knowing* that by the time you get to the casino to play them, you have already learned what these games are, what they pay, how they pay it, and how to play them. That alone saves you a lot of money, and a great deal of learning that you otherwise would have to do only after arriving in the casino. And, if you have picked up this book on the way out of the casino—perhaps on your way home after you have spent your vacation—now you have something to ponder and something to look forward to on your next trip. Share this information with your friends, because they too will benefit from information that is vitally important if they are to have not only a fun trip, but also a winning trip.

There are many definitions of "winning." To the pure gambler, winning means going home with more money than the amount with which you arrived. But there aren't many pure gamblers, and most of us—according to my own research—fall into the other 99% of casino players: those commonly referred to as "recreational players." Even those of us who may be "semi-professional gamblers" fall into the category of recreational players, because gambling is not our sole source of income. Naturally, there are different levels to these categories. Some of us are more "semi-professional gamblers" than "recreational players." I would put myself in the former category. While it is certain that these days I don't do as much of it as I used to, mostly because my business commitments eat up so much of my time, nevertheless I still find opportunities whenever possible to spend as much time in the casinos as I can. But the days of the 24/7 lifestyle have now become mostly part of my youth, rather than of my present. I am far from being an "old fossil," but I have now become closer to the broader definition of "recreational player" than I was in the past. This, then, makes me appreciate even more the approach that most people take to their casino gaming.

Since I live in Las Vegas, I have access to a casino on a daily basis within a few minutes of my home. I can go at any time, for as long as I want to—short time, or long time—and when I'm done I can come home and stay at home for as long as I want to and then go back to the casino on a moment's notice, or even a whim. This access makes it possible for me to practice dedicated gaming, either for the purpose of generating income or for entertainment.

But I realize that many people don't live in Las Vegas. They come here—or to any other gaming center—only a few times a year, and primarily for the purpose of entertainment. Even if you visit your local casino, or the casino which is nearest to where you live, on a regular basis, for most people it still requires a trip. Naturally, those who live in Las Vegas, Reno, Atlantic City, or any other casino center understand that proximity allows for more wide-ranging choices and abilities than are available to those who have to travel some distance in order to participate in this activity. If only because of this necessity to "travel to get there," the majority of players in this category are "recreational" players. There is absolutely nothing wrong with that, because—after all—the reason why you come is for recreation. The fact that your recreation includes visits to the casino, where you can play slots, is a bonus. And, if you know which slots to select and how to play them before you get to the casino, this recreational activity can not only be more entertaining, but also many times more rewarding.

These days when I play as a recreational player I am no longer looking to make that "big score" for which I had looked in the past. I like to play the slots as much for their entertainment value as for the profitability. This does not mean, of course, that I walk into the casino blindly and simply stick my money into whatever happens to be there. Being empowered with knowledge means being empowered with the ability to choose where to spend your money, and that is a powerful incentive indeed. Instead of blindly sticking your money in any slot machine that you happen to be passing by, now you have the opportunity to find out more about these games and then put your money in with the knowledge necessary to make the game perform to its optimum advantage.

Your objective should always be to have fun, and to enjoy the experience to the fullest. This may—or may not—involve winning money. If it does, so much the better, but if it doesn't, it should not spoil your experience. If you feel really bad about losing money, the first thing you should do is question your approach to the game. Did you pick the right game? Do you know why you picked that game? Did you know how the game plays? Did you know what the pays were, and how they had to be achieved in order to win something? Did you have the correct goals and perspective? Were you expecting too much? Were you expecting too much relative to how much you were willing to invest? Generally, did you empower yourself with knowledge in order to avoid failure?

These questions may or may not apply to you. I know from personal experience that some of them apply to me, and others do not. And, of course, these are only a few of the many hundreds of questions that we ask to relate to our experiences and the expectations we may have brought with us prior to these experiences. If we expect too much, we rarely achieve that goal, and then we tend to be disappointed. Conversely, if we set our goals too low, we will not feel satisfied when we have achieved them, or exceeded them. We then tend to push for higher achievements, without having first set those higher goals; and that may lead to additional disappointments.

Whether we win or lose depends equally on us and on the machine. You have to remember that slot machines are manufactured in a way in which they are mathematically predetermined always to win money for the casino. That's a fact, and a fact of life. We have to deal with it. But that doesn't mean that the machines do not pay. If the slot machine never paid, no one would play it. That is also a fact. Therefore, the way to achieve the best value, avoid disappointment, and maximize your potential for winning entertainment is first to understand all of this, and then to empower yourself with the knowledge that will help you navigate all of these choices, and to objectively set reasonable goals that are reasonably achievable. That way you will never feel disappointed, because even if you did not manage to make that big win, at least you know that you gave yourself the best chance to win. You can therefore be justifiably proud of the way you approached your casino gaming and slot machine playing experience.

Most of us tend to remember our winning sessions more than losing ones. If you ever have an opportunity to talk to a professional gambler, or a semi-professional gambler, the first thing they will tell you is this: "It's a tough way to make an easy living." The second thing they will tell you is that they remember their *losing* sessions a lot more vividly than the winning ones. This is different from the "regular" gamblers, or "recreational" players, who will tend to remember the winning sessions more than the losing ones. That is colloquially known as "lying into your own pocket." It afflicts most people, and we therefore have to be conscious of it if we are to overcome it. Long ago, I learned to focus more on *losing* sessions than winning ones because there are lessons to be learned from the times you lose. This is because I *expect* winning sessions, based on knowledge and experience, and if I don't have a winning session then I concentrate on this, and analyze the situation in order to learn from it, so that next time I will avoid the errors that caused the losing session in the first place. And, if I determine that I did nothing incorrectly, then I can confidently apply this to the variances in mathematical probability—more commonly known as "a run of bad luck"—and rest easy knowing that I did all that was humanly possible to approach the game, and situation, with the proper mindset and control over my own gaming destiny.

Our approach to playing slot machines, consequently, should be one of knowledge, personal stability, and the balance between what we "hope" to achieve and what is *reasonably achievable*. It is the striking of this balance that separates the winners from the losers, not just in slot machine, or casino gambling, but in life in general. Optimism cultured with knowledge tempered by experience equal success.

And that is the philosophy behind all of my books, including this one.

Good luck, and I wish you the best of success!

Victor H. Royer
Las Vegas
April 2010

Acknowledgments

No man or woman is an island. All human beings are part of a group, a collective, called the human race. We are interdependent, some more than others, and some of us more directly upon each other. I have now written 22 books on casino games and gaming and more than 100 reports for the gaming industry. I have written about 1,000 gaming columns over the past 26 years, as well as many other writing exploits. And I continue to do it to this day. That's a lot of writing. While it is true that the world of the writer is a lonely one, and that I sit at my desk for long hours, weeks, months, and even years to make a book a reality, it is also a fact that none of this is purely a solitary effort.

To write a book like this one takes a team of people on whom I rely for much of the information that makes the writing possible. Yes, I do have personal experiences with these games, and much of what I write is directly applicable to these experiences, and how I play in the casinos. But there are other situations, and facts, such as the game's percentages, details, designs, photos, and so on—including rights and permissions from the owners of the copyrights and trademarks—that I alone could not compile. For this, therefore, I am grateful to a number of people, all of whom have contributed to this book.

First and foremost, I wish to thank the Executives and Staff of Aristocrat Technologies Inc., Las Vegas, USA, for their help and cooperation in providing me access to their games. This also extends to their Australian parent company, Aristocrat Technologies

Australia Pty Limited. Specifically, I wish to thank the following: Nick Khin, Doug Fallon, Dona Cassese, Seamus McGill, Julie Witherby, Tom Smock, Susan Heiman, Jeremy Fenderson, Don Pitchford, Alison Barnett, Karen Mercier, Ted Hase and Angela Abshier.

And, to all the Aristocrat team members around the globe for creating the games that players love to play.

Personal Thanks

In addition to all of the wonderful people at Aristocrat, many others have been with me for a long time, and I also wish to acknowledge their contributions.

Ms. Ann LaFarge, my editor. Ann is the person who makes my writing look so good, by her brilliance as Chief Editor. Ann has edited most of my books, those from my publisher in New York, and this book as well. I am eternally grateful to this wonderful lady, and for her talents. I am very proud to have her as my editor.

Ms. Anne Gillis, my chief designer. She is the brilliant lady whose design talents made it possible for my manuscript to become the book you are now reading. She, and her team, are responsible for making everything fit, all of the photos to be sized and printed properly and legibly, and for everything that goes into the production aspects of creating a book. It is her skill in these areas that makes it possible for me to write these books, because I know that they will be designed with flair and brilliance and that, therefore, the published book will look as good as it possibly can be made.

Mr. Neil Mummery, and family. My best and oldest friend, from Australia. Neil lives in Melbourne, and for the next three years will be one of the executives at Exxon-Mobil in Papua New Guinea. His friendship spans the decades, and the oceans. Without his faith, and friendship, I would not have been around to write this book. My appreciation goes out to him, and my love to his family.

Mr. Larry Levit, my CPA. And my friend, and advisor. His friendship, and excellence as a CPA, have kept me grounded, and in step with the changing landscape of finance. I am very grateful to him for all his efforts on my behalf.

Mr. Michael Harrison, Attorney at Law. My attorney, and my friend. For three decades, his steadfast help, and commitment to me and my business interests have made me secure in the knowledge that we can handle any obstacle. His skills as corporate attorney have made my business interests stronger, and more viable.

And my dear Mom, Mrs. Georgina Royer. All that I am, and everything that is in my books, articles, and all that I can achieve, are all due to her. She has been my foundation, my friend, my guide, confidante, and force of reason and balance all my life. Her life has been extraordinary, and her accomplishments mind-boggling. As a brilliant and highly educated professional—at a time when women were not considered to be capable executives—she was already well-respected, and ahead of her time. All of her colleagues marveled at how she could solve problems and issues, and prevent other problems and issues from happening. And this was in the 1930s and 1940s. Think of it. And, it was in Europe. She survived the Nazis, she survived the Communists, and she survived a life of hardship the likes of which you can't even imagine. And she did all of this with grace, determination, and unfailing commitment to me. How can I ever repay this? Never. But that is not the point, is it? Such dedication and commitment can only be repaid with love and respect. And so, my darling Mom, I send this to you here, in this book. With all my love!

May there be life, peace, and happiness for us all.

Copyrights and Trademarks

"Aristocrat, its game names, product names and logos are all trademarks or registered trademarks of Aristocrat Technologies Australia Pty Limited."

- JAWS: JAWS and JAWS Night Hunter are trademarks and copyright of Universal Studios. Licensed by Universal Studios Licensing LLLP. All Rights Reserved.
- THE SOPRANOS: © Home Box Office, Inc. All Rights Reserved. THE SOPRANOS, HBO, RESPECT THE BING and THIS THING OF OURS are trademarks or registered trademarks of Home Box Office, Inc.
- KENTUCKY DERBY: © Churchill Downs Incorporated. KENTUCKY DERBY, RUN FOR THE ROSES and OAKS DAY are trademarks or registered trademarks of Churchill Downs Incorporated. All Rights Reserved.
- GOLDEN AXE™ GOLDEN AXE™ is a trademark of SEGA Corporation. ©SEGA
- BONANZA BROS.™ BONANZA BROS.™ is a trademark of SEGA Corporation. © SEGA
- JEFF FOXWORTHY: JEFF FOXWORTHY™, REDNECK RUMBLE™ are trademarks or registered trademarks of Jeff Foxworthy.
- ZORRO: ©2008 Zorro Productions, Inc. All Rights Reserved.
- POKERPRO is a registered trademark of PokerTek Inc. Corporation North Carolina.

Author's Statement

All of the information and text written in this book has been created by the Author of this book and, as such, all of the opinions, expressions, text, prose, statements, advice, gaming advice, discussions, and any other written words that are part of this book are the sole opinions and creation of the Author, and as such are limited only to the Author, and therefore do not necessarily represent the opinions of Aristocrat Technologies Inc., USA, or Aristocrat Technologies Australia Pty Limited, or Kentucky Derby, Jeff Foxworthy, HBO, Sega, or Universal, or any of its (their) subsidiaries, licensees, vendors and/or assigns.

No part of this book is to be construed as promoting gambling, or any other forms of gaming, such as may be socially or legally inappropriate, or outside of the regulated jurisdictions of any State, or Nation, or locale. No liability is hereby accepted for any misuse or misunderstanding by any person, persons, entities, businesses, governments, or any other uses by any person, persons, governments and/or entities whatsoever, outside of the scope and purpose of this book, and its intended purpose as an educational and instructional work of Author's opinion.